The Best Worst Time of Your Life:

Four Practices to Get You Through the Pain of Divorce

Hang in there Brandy...

Allison Sleight and

Andrea Hipps, LBSW, Certified Divorce Coach®

The Best Worst Time of Your Life

ISBN: 9-798-7325735-2-7

Praise for *The Best Worst Time of Your Life*

If you are looking for a guide who is real, practical, humorous and full of hard-earned wisdom, then Andrea is your guide. Andrea distills what she learned in her own process and her relentless pursuit of answers in both an emotionally honest and hopeful way. She doesn't minimize the intense pain of divorce and at the same time she finds the unexpected gifts that come from "working with your breaking and not against it."

~ Kristen Bell, co-author of the award-winning New York Times
Bestselling book *Zimzum of Love* and regular teacher on the RobCast

If you have always wondered how to go about your divorce in a way that works for everyone in the family, even your spouse, this book is the one to read. In over 40 years as a family law attorney, I have never run across a book that talked about the hard parts of divorce. Clearly Andrea has been there. I am privileged in that Andrea is now not only a colleague, but also a former client of mine. I witnessed firsthand the choices she made during her own divorce that allowed her to enjoy her post-divorce family with real freedom. The process she describes works for everyone, but particularly for children. You only get one chance to write the story of your divorce. Every child of divorced parents tells others about how they experienced their parents' divorce. Sometimes those discussions are with friends, or spouses, or sometimes counselors. There are no "do-overs." Use this book as a guide as you start this journey or even if you are in the middle of that difficult journey. The journey is never easy, but this book will help you make the tough decisions.

~ Randall Velzen, Past President of the Grand Rapids Bar Association,
Founding Member of Collaborative Divorce Professionals of West Michigan,
Past President of the Collaborative Practice Institute of Michigan, and Guest
Lecturer at the International Academy of Collaborative Professionals

This book was an amazing read. I could not put it down. Much needed insights. A must read for anyone contemplating or going through a divorce. It does my heart good to know that the author, Andrea, is in the business of making the process of divorce a little kinder and gentler, especially when there are children.

~ Randall R. Cooper, MBA, Supreme Court of Florida Certified Family Mediator, Member of the International Collaborative for Credentialed Divorce Practitioners®, Credentialed Divorce Practitioner, CDP® Registry member, Certified Divorce Financial Analyst, CDFA®

Andrea's wisdom ignites **LIFE!** *These words will help you reimagine and create a new and positive future for yourself. I wish I had found such a clear roadmap 20 years ago when I started the single parent pathway. Her commitment to positive co-parenting is refreshing and she gives readers a clear "how to" even in a dark and difficult situation. No matter where you are in the journey, this book is a must!!*

~ Tammy G. Daughtry / Founder, CoParenting International

Dedicated to Harper and Hadley
and to Todd

Table of Contents

Chapter 1 – I'm Sorry You Find Yourself Reading This Book 1

Chapter 2 – The Present Moment
(And Other Places You Don't Want to Be). 23

Chapter 3 – You Need A New Triangle. 45

Chapter 4 – Change Versus Transition. 61

Chapter 5 – Practice 1: Rise Above. 79

Chapter 6 – Practice 2: Own Your Part 99

Chapter 7 – Practice 3: Fight For Gratitude 117

Chapter 8 – Practice 4: Say Yes 139

Chapter 9 – What Remains 159

About The Author 170

More Support. 171

Stay Connected 171

Acknowledgments 172

Chapter 1

I'm Sorry You Find Yourself Reading This Book

I'm sorry you find yourself reading this book. Going through a divorce—wanted or unwanted—is plainly put, horrific. It rips at everything in you, destroys everything you once held sacred, and incites a fear of the future that is at times completely paralyzing. You feel terribly alone, rejected, angry (really angry), overwhelmed, sad, and defeated. Your basic habits, once reliable repetitions in your day, have now evaporated. Things like remembering your schedule, eating at normal times, and caring about life in general are all now hard to grasp in your once fairly pulled together world.

If you feel like you are dying, you are on to something. Part of you certainly is.

I wrote this book for you. I wrote it because the hardest part of divorce is often the part that happens before everybody knows. It happens in the quiet and loud discussions with your partner that start to reveal a tear in the fabric of your togetherness. You examine the tear, and you work at repairing it, but sometimes you wake up after all of that effort and notice that the tear is really more of a rip. You might not feel sure if your feverish sewing is really pulling any of the frays back together.

1

My Boo-Hoo Crew: Mom, Sisters, aunts, neighbor,
Rs presidency, Bishop W.

The Best Worst Time of Your Life

In the days, weeks, months, and sometimes years before your divorce is made public, you identify the small handful of people whom you can trust to walk with you through this. These are your people—your "boo-hoo crew," as I call them. You probably have one. Even if it's just your mom or a co-worker. If you're lucky, it's your forever friends. These people hold the light for you when you can't. They listen as you go on (and on and on) about the injustice, the shock, the fear, and the reluctance. They hear your worry about your kids. They tell you that you're worth fighting for and convince you to keep fighting for yourself when the pressure simply overtakes you.

While this small, faithful group holds your hand, you look for books and blogs and resources—anything that will tell you what to do next. The writings that you find tell you some fairly helpful things. Get a lawyer, get a therapist, put your kids first, speak kindly about your spouse. Basically, move through it and move on. And you know they are right, in part. You know you will need to do those things.

And then you likely seek out a friend, or a friend of a friend, who is already divorced. It's a club you don't want to be in, but you know you need to meet with someone who gets it. You need to look someone in the eye who has walked this road. And that person will also tell you some helpful things. It's rough, they say. Take care of yourself. Get a really good lawyer. You listen as they tell their stories of loss, and you may become an ear for their story even as you process your own.

But no one seems to be able to answer the every day (and every night) question:

How will I get through this?

Not the "how" of the process itself—the lawyers, the mediators, telling your families, the child-sharing plans, the weekends

2

back and forth, the separation of belongings, the establishment of financial support. Not that how. I'm talking about the harder how.

When I was moving through my divorce, there wasn't a book that could speak to how I was to cope with the absolute destruction of heart, body, mind, and soul that accompanies a divorce. Maybe some top-level materials spoke about it like it was a pretty big bump in the road, but nothing really attempted to put into words what I should do with the weight of the feelings that I went to bed with and woke up with day after day. Nothing helped me normalize the exhaustion, worry, overwhelm, indigestion, lack of eating, overeating, hollowness, fatigue, rage, shame, and numbness that could happen all in the course of one week, one day.

There wasn't any guidance on how to have a productive conversation with the person who no longer wants to live life with you. There was no advice about how to manage the rage of trying, and failing, to simply come to agreement on the small pieces of separation. There were no suggestions about how to speak kindly when yet another miscommunication occurs. How was I to face this humiliating event and keep fixing dinner and making sure birthdays get recognized?

Couldn't someone talk honestly about the breaking?

I trust that your boo-hoo crew, your books, and your divorced friends will get you through your external logistics. Those are hard, but you can trace the path of many who have walked before you. These pages are my attempt to help you get through your internal mess and start working with your breaking, instead of against it. It is my heartfelt effort at putting to words the great undoing you are going through and shedding a small light on where you might go next in your efforts to heal. These words won't make your pain go away. They may not even make it subside any faster. But I hope they will be a companion. And I hope they will help shape your heart and your life in these dark days. Because I'm a firm believer that your daily efforts, made in the right direction, will lead to the hope and healing and closure you seek right now.

You should know that I also wrote this book for me. It started as an effort to report back to myself what I went through during my own divorce: how I survived, how I navigated the changing relationship with my former spouse, and how I got to where I am now. I initially viewed it as a past tense account, but something interesting happened as I started writing. My life and the effects of my divorce kept unfolding in real time. When I wanted to be writing in hindsight, I found myself still writing in the moment. As I wrote, I had to look in the mirror and see that despite my hard work and my successes, I was not yet the woman that I hoped to become. I had too easily accepted that I would probably never get to the point where my divorce did not deeply affect me in my daily life. I counseled my divorced friends that they might not get to this point either. Don't get me wrong, we need to remind each other that it's ok to be affected. It wasn't about getting rid of the situation, it was about allowing it to be a teacher and learning to live well *with* it, not against it. For me, it was also about making the conscious effort to put myself in a mental and emotional position to move on.

I can tell you, and my friends will agree, that my divorce certainly affects me differently and in a less stinging way now. It will ask for the spotlight for a while and then it will recede into the shadows, only to come forward once again. I resist it taking center stage almost every time. I return to these questions over and over: what would it look like to sway with that back-and-forth rhythm of light and shadow instead of pushing the spotlight away? How could I allow the times of spotlight to be a teacher, not an interruption? How could I somehow anticipate and not fear when those spotlight moments come back again and again?

And now, after thinking through these questions, after waiting for and recognizing the invitation to truly move on, there is no more back and forth. There's a continuity between dark and spotlight that isn't so destabilizing. My story has changed, and I believe your story can birth another one too.

I also wrote this book for my kids. Their dad and I have been very careful with the story of our relationship as it pertains to our girls. We both want warm, full-hearted, meaningful relationships with them, and we don't want the harder parts of our dissolution story to alienate either one of us from them. They have questions, just like your kids do, and this book will answer a few of them. Frankly, their dad and I probably have just as many questions as they do. Our kids know it is not their fault, but they also don't get how the two great parents that they love could end up divorced. As parents, we know that raising emotionally healthy kids through a transition of this magnitude takes courage.

I also wrote this book to tell you the story of how God came close to me during this awful time, and a divine presence loved me and changed me. What I learned and the reflections I can offer back to you now generate from the kindness of God's heart toward me in those years. I was given the desire to do divorce differently and to land in a place that wouldn't leave me feeling jaded and resentful. I knew that if my marriage was going to make it, then I was going to have a great marriage. If my marriage was going to end in divorce, then I was going to have a great divorce. What I would not accept was a crummy marriage or an ugly divorce.

5

God pulled me near, so even while I raged, I was comforted. While I resisted, there was patience being offered to me. While I broke, there was mending being done behind the scenes. And all along the way, I kept sensing the encouragement to walk toward the vision of something more beautiful and brighter than what I could produce myself. It was a place where I didn't need to win and where revenge wasn't the highest aim. It was a place where the wounding stopped. It didn't have a shape, it just had a pull.

I also wrote this book for my clients. For over 20 years, my career has been directed toward helping build housing communities that are affordable, beautiful, and meet the needs of low-income and homeless people in my community. This work has produced hundreds of affordable housing units for the most vulnerable among us and led to revitalization in the neighborhoods around them. I had no idea that the same drive to protect, care for, revitalize, and make homes for these individuals and families would evolve into my current divorce coaching business. The same impulse that fueled my community development efforts is now shaping my work with a different population.

As a divorce coach, I witness that divorce leads to a homelessness of heart for many of us and a deterioration of spirit. My own divorce story, both the lows and the highs, have connected me with many like-minded women and men who are tired of not feeling at home in their post-divorce life. They are tired of living with psychological static around the topic of their former partner and the debris that litters their mental front yard. They crave revitalization like I did. This book is for all of the stories I have had the privilege to coach so far and the many I will hear in the future.

The words you will read are my invitation to take your divorce recovery to a deeper place. Divorce is a painful, destabilizing, and crushing experience of family life. The way we traditionally go about it (with parents who struggle to deal with their own grief and rage, kids who suffer under the strain of their emotionally taxed parents, and the tensions between mom and dad persisting years after the legal process is complete) is now contributing to a public health crisis. Like you, I would love for divorce to not exist. I send out deep gratitude to my fellow colleagues who are therapists or marriage and family counselors, knowing that they labor with struggling couples to make sure that divorce is not the first option. But the time has come for us to accept that divorce is a key player in family life, and to work to set a new standard for how it can unfold. If you have to do it, do it better. And if you're serious about it, this book will challenge you to start the exploration.

At the end of each chapter, you'll find "Questions For Your Deepening." These are designed to help you integrate what you're reading, cast light on the pieces of your own divorce narrative that need new material, and start to shape a new way of processing and healing. The growth will be deeper if you can put pen to paper with your answers. One last note: I am a female who experienced divorce in a heterosexual marriage, but my conviction is that these truths go across boundaries of gender and sexual orientation. They are human at their core, and useful for anyone in or leaving a partnered relationship.

HOW IT ALL STARTED

Make no mistake, while I enjoy a great deal of freedom around my divorce story now, it wasn't pretty in the beginning. I remember vividly the night my husband, Mr. H, said he wanted to start talking about what it would look like for us to raise our kids in two different homes. We had been married for about 13 years, and this was not a dreamy conversation about buying a second family home to return to year after year.

This was divorce.

His home.

My home.

I cannot fully express to you the hysteria that took root in my heart at that moment. Fight or flight kicked in, and I couldn't pick between them. So I did both. And right away. First, I fought. And after the fighting words got quieter, I thought I should take flight. I lived in West Michigan at the time, which meant that snow was a daily part of winter life, and not the novelty it was when I lived in Arizona. It unfortunately also meant that taking flight that night was slowed by the putting on of a layered winter costume: boots, then coat, scarf, gloves, and hat.

My flight consisted of taking a walk that cold, snowy night. I had no destination in mind when I closed the door behind me. My stomach was literally shriveling inside of me as I started out, my heart ached with a heaviness that couldn't be sustained. I prayed that God would make it all go away and also knew that it probably would not go away. I crossed the street and walked down to a neighbor's home maybe 10 houses down from mine. I could see that they were hosting some mutual friends at their home that night for dinner. Even though both couples were dear family friends of ours, something in me couldn't walk up to the door and ask for help. I didn't even understand what kind of help I needed. I couldn't translate into words the experience I was having—which was that my life was shutting down without my permission, and I wasn't sure I was going to make it through the night. It wasn't that I would take my own life, it was that the

8

pain was too overwhelming to bear. It felt as though my body had submitted its resignation letter. It could no longer conduct business. I seriously thought I would die of my own broken heart.

In my decidedly irrational mind, I decided then and there that I needed to die where someone could identify me to the police. So, continuing on this irrational path, I laid down in the snow on the sidewalk in front of their home. And I waited to die. I really did. No one came walking down the sidewalk that night, though I often wonder how a passerby would have responded and equally wondered what I would have said in return. At some point, I got up. I realized that I was not going to be spared this pain. I was going to have to walk home in the pain and face whatever came next.

It comforts me to know that science backs me up on the degree of stress and intensity that swirled around my experience of divorce. In the late 1960's, researchers Thomas Holmes and Richard Rahe sought to explore the relationship between our health and our stressful life events. What they discovered after combing through the medical histories of over 5,000 patients was that a noticeable correlation did in fact exist. They went on to establish the Holmes and Rahe Stress Scale, still in use today, which assigns weighted values to stressful events. Combining the cumulative scores from stressful events experienced by a person in a given year can essentially anticipate that person's prospects for future illness. Not surprisingly, the death of a spouse or child is ranked as the most stressful life event on their scale, with a score of 100. Second in line is divorce, with a score of 73. Loss, it seems, weighs heavy on the figurative heart as well as the actual heart.

My own sense of loss started innocently enough. A year and a half before my snowy, desperate walk, our family was celebrating the second birthday of my youngest daughter. Grandparents were in attendance, and her great-great aunt and uncle made a special trip with cousins as well. After the festivities, Mr. H and I ended up in one of those raise-your-voices-this-is-going-nowhere arguments. At one point, he uttered a short and calm statement that was my first whiff of the loss to come:

Some part of me has disconnected from you, and I am not sure if I can get it back.

He went on to say he was "done" with my anger. I spent a very small moment in shock and then, of course, went straight to anger. What else could I do at that point? I fixated on our interchange. Disconnected from me? Are you allowed to do that? What does that even mean? Do you hate me? Are you even trying to get it back? How did you lose it? What is "it" anyway? He didn't know. He was pretty quiet after that statement. His silence didn't speak volumes; it said very little and offered nothing that I could immediately interpret.

This infuriated me. It drove me crazy. If he had said he wanted us to work on it, that would have at least given me some hope. If he had explained that he didn't know what to do with certain behaviors of mine that were killing him, it would have shed some light on the situation. There wasn't anything though. No explanation was offered, just a dispassionate notice that his body would live next to mine, but that his heart was no longer my home. It was a notice of eviction. But as evictions go, it was like I was being kicked out just to the front yard. Kicked out of his emotional house? Yes. Out of his life? Not yet.

Cue the freak out. It should be said that my personality is driven by two things: the love of control and the fear of losing it. So Mr. H's "Proclamation of Disconnection," as I refer to it now, triggered me into overdrive. It felt as though someone had taken over control of my entire future. This is not a time to sit idly by, I thought. Threats abound! I must rally!

My head and heart were scrambling. In reality, though, the Proclamation was followed by a cold, snowy winter of more quiet. It was dark. We were confused. We would travel separately out to our hot tub in the evening after the girls were asleep, surrounded by mounds of white snow. I would stare at him. He would stare at the trees. At times I pleaded for more information, a suggestion of what to do, a hint at what comes next. But it was honestly just pretty quiet. He seemed like he didn't know what to say. I felt tremendous frustration that I had somehow led us to this point, but I had no inkling of what to do to walk us back.

The quiet was compounded not only by our just having moved to Michigan with starter friendships still not yet proven, but also by the fact that he was a pastor. A new pastor. At a big church. One that wouldn't likely look favorably on their leader withdrawing from his marriage. While it wasn't asked of me, I found myself keeping this new quiet season of us entirely secret from these new friends. I think that impulse was partly driven by the instinct to protect him from losing his job. I was a stay-at-home mother, and my financial stability was inextricably linked to his success. But I think the greater part of me willing to stay silent was driven by my own unwillingness to even accept that what was happening was real. My denial was firmly intact.

This chosen isolation from new Michigan friends was balanced out by my complete freedom to share the entirety of the drama with my old Phoenix, Arizona friends. We had moved away only months before, so our intimacy as friends was still going strong. They felt perplexed along with me. They held my story, but they were also aware that they only held half of the overall story. You see, not only was Mr. H silent with me, he was also relatively silent with our friends.

This was about to change in the summer of 2011, when we found ourselves traveling to a conference in Pittsburgh where Mr. H would be speaking. He was the keynote speaker at the national convention of our denomination, a convention that would be attended by many of our Phoenix friends. I felt very hopeful in the build up to that event. It was the City of Bridges! Surely we could be inspired to build one. Finally, we would be face to face with people who knew us, loved us, and could speak into this wild moment in which we found ourselves. I was confident that we would leave that event with some hope for our reconnection.

I was wrong, so very wrong.

Instead of building a bridge, the event exposed all of the structural damage, and the deterioration was apparent to all three of the Phoenix couple friends present with us. At one dinner where I think each one of us still holds some ache of regret, it seemed like everyone took a turn challenging him. They were as stumped as I was about his new position toward me. They tried to lovingly hold him accountable for this new behavior of retreating into himself. They wondered aloud what was taking shape. To him, it felt like an attack. To me, it felt like I was no longer alone. Finally, out of the long winter of silence, I was now surrounded by 6 other people cheering for me, for us, for possibility! Six other people were as shocked as I was that we were in this unfamiliar place and wanted to see us figure it out. If we all agreed something was wrong with him, then majority wins! Something is wrong with him! He has to change! See? We all knew it, or so I thought.

But the drive home from Pittsburgh revealed to me that we had not built the bridge for which I had longed. In fact, we probably burnt a bit of the one we were still standing on. That six-hour car ride home was marked by phrases I never thought I would hear. He was not willing to commit to our future. He had no comment about what it meant to step outside of the commitment to our vows. I was grief-stricken. It simply could not be true. My denial was rooted.

THE CHALLENGES

After the convention, the wife of one of the couples passed through Michigan and stayed with us for a few days. She had brought her two daughters with her, and their presence was a comfort like no other. While my friend's daughters played with mine, she and I dove into strategy sessions about how to situate myself more comfortably in this painfully uncomfortable time. Her spiritual and emotional guidance provided the first marching orders to help focus my struggling heart in crucial ways.

She offered a number of challenges that were unique to me and what I needed to learn in my situation. They weren't necessarily challenges that she would issue to everyone or that I would even issue to you; they were spoken into my own set of limitations and growth areas. I would venture that some of you may even need to work with challenges that are the complete opposite of these. For me, though, this is where I needed to start. I'll offer more universal guidance in later chapters.

First Challenge: No Catastrophizing

Up until her challenge, catastrophizing was a beloved way of life for me. At times it still is, albeit in a way that I can recognize and address more quickly now. But back then, imagining things to be worse than they really were was a habit of mind to which I regularly turned. I think it was really an attempt to find the edge of the pain. If I could identify and explain just how much was going to go wrong, just how much control I was losing, then maybe I could start to make sense of what was happening. It was also an attempt to shock myself out of denial. Things are at stake! Really bad stuff is about to happen! Wake up! Freak out! If I could just freak out far enough, then maybe I could make sense of my terrible life circumstances. Spoiler alert: I never made sense of it.

The catastrophizing and freaking out never made sense of *anything* for me. It didn't lead to peace. It never answered the questions that were being added daily to my list. Underneath it was really just a plea for the universe to recognize what I perceived to be my complete inability to face reality and function well in it. I genuinely believed that I couldn't handle it. And catastrophizing helped me voice that deep fear.

Committing to this first challenge required a complete renovation of my classic hysteria protocol. Instead of hearing something from Mr. H, freaking out inside and outside about it, and imagining everything that was going to go wrong, it was an invitation to take each comment from him as it was, to stay calm, and to stay present. It meant not going too far into the future. It meant exercising the discipline of showing up. It meant showing up when it was easier to leave the conversation and disengage from relating at all. It meant I would keep talking, keep listening, and keep working on it. I had to engage with the situation as it was, not how I catastrophized it to be.

I cannot overstate how crucial this step is in handling the gigantic life bomb that a possible divorce can be in your life. And while it can take years to learn to stop catastrophizing about your own set of unique circumstances, the process cannot get started without your intention. And that intention can be the hardest work of all to initiate.

Second Challenge: Consider Mr. H's Happiness First

I am an only child. While this means that I enjoy the confidence and self-esteem typically associated with only children, it also means I didn't grow up with a lot of interference when it came to what I wanted. I envy my own kids now when I think about all of the ways that they are so naturally learning to put someone else before themselves, yield to the needs and desires of another, and participate in a give and take relationship model simply by living in a home with a sibling. My first college roommate still likes to joke with me that she was the first person to teach me that I had to share the oxygen in our room. I'd be lying if I didn't say there was some truth to that!

As an only child, my happiness was continuously indulged without any other players to create resistance. I share this with you to explain that the challenge to consider Mr. H's happiness first—guidance that I'm pretty sure is on the first page of any marriage handbook—was an idea that required concerted effort.

It's easy to look at my ten years of married life with Mr. H up to this point and make a strong case that I did put his happiness first. After we met in college in Texas, I happily chose to move to his hometown in Minnesota, forgoing my own graduate school opportunity, so that we could be together while he got his start in the advertising industry for four years. When leaving advertising for seminary, I was all in to move to Los Angeles and support him in his studies for four more years. Seminary led to pastoring, and I enthusiastically moved to Phoenix for a five-year adventure in ministry there. Our final stop as a married couple took us to West Michigan to continue in ministry at a different church. This was the move I was probably most hesitant to make, but it proved to be full of the best people to hold my heart during its breaking and remaking process.

So, I did care about his happiness. I'm not that remedial in my understanding of the first rule of marriage. It's just that I think it is easy for people to look at that path of many years and many addresses and think that I really sacrificed a great deal to make sure Mr. H could achieve his many goals. And while I do agree that I wanted him to succeed, it wasn't a huge sacrifice to make those moves. The bottom line was that all of those moves across the country made *me* happy too. I was personally eager to move in every situation. I'm a person who loves people, diving into them, understanding them, and living life with them. I like making home, and I like change. But my first two loves will forever be intensity and projects. I'm unique, I know, but the intensity of planning a possible move, the move itself, and the years of adjustment afterward has always been a welcome experience. Moving is marked by projects like packing, getting new furniture, and setting up utilities—and I enjoy every minute spent on these tasks. What better companion for his multi-city life could Mr. H have than me? I became known for my ability to have rooms arranged and wall hangings up within the first weekend of our arrival at a new address.

It should also be noted that up until his Proclamation of Disconnection, I was under the impression that what *I* had wanted out of life so far was also what *he* wanted. There weren't a lot of places where I understood us to be on opposite sides of an issue requiring either of us to consider sacrificing.

When my friend suggested putting him first with intention, or at least considering his needs more deliberately, it was a new conscious exercise for me. It pulled me back from the larger big picture of "yes I will leave these people and move across the country with you" toward something less macro. Daily, I began to think first about how I could make Mr. H happy. I started to put his happiness before my own, sacrifice myself for his gain, spend less time preserving myself, and pay less attention to securing my own happiness.

After some time putting forth effort toward these two challenges, I noticed some pretty major mental shifts in me. First, I realized just how *much* I catastrophize and think only about myself! Within a few days of operating within this framework, I felt exposed. My heart could really see the degree to which I struggled in these two areas. It was equally empowering and disheartening. On one hand I felt powerful. I felt as though I could live more and more from this place to the extent that I would gain the ability to influence Mr. H and woo him back from the silence we had learned to inhabit.

Eliminating the catastrophizing made me work harder than ever at making the relationship work. Catastrophizing was a bad habit that only blew things up; it didn't build anything. The world-ending comments I was making didn't get us anywhere except to desperation. It put me squarely in the future, and not attending to the actual moment. If our thoughts create our feelings, I got my first glimpse of what it meant to exercise control over your thoughts as a matter of self-care.

Thinking about Mr. H's happiness was also a big reveal. Since having children, particularly, I rarely consciously considered his happiness. My own life was lived in such service to the kids, I felt like I was always the one deserving and needing some sort of relief. Unfortunately, with my limited skillset at the time, I believed that my relief was supposed to come from Mr. H. Naturally, he failed at giving me what I need, mostly because it wasn't his job to do so. It caused me great pain to see how difficult I made his life when I refused his simple requests for time off as well. There was very little freedom I could give him with joy—I gave the freedom, but it was always with reluctance. Entering into a "whatever Mr. H needs to be happy" mode was amazing, because I was truly able to give it. There was a strength rising in me that ended up allowing me to become capable to handle the life I lived after I let him go.

I was starting to get a glimpse of my own capacity independent of Mr. H. One of the gifts of marriage is the ability to share the burden of life's work with each other. However, one of the unfortunate consequences of marrying young (22 years old) was that I never truly experienced the level to which I could carry my life on my own. I went from being my parents' dependent to being his dependent. I missed that important stage of independence. I now found myself being sent back a life grade or two to learn this part. Capacity building in my own heart freed me to not need him, in a healthy way. Yes, we were married. But we were still two separate people. This helped me to emotionally disconnect enough to give him some freedom.

The lack of catastrophizing coupled with thinking first of Mr. H's needs resulted in the bottom line of me just showing up. I noted how many times the discomfort of our life caused me to leave emotionally or ignore our reality. I remembered being annoyed when he wanted to try to work on us in some way. Now it felt different, and showing up like this took work. Living through the pain, and giving to him despite the pain, took a great deal of focus.

I ended up operating in this "showing up framework" for months, checking in with my friend periodically. I had an overwhelming sense that I was waking up. I was contributing building blocks to my marriage for the first time in a long time. I felt so very proud of my contribution and grateful that the desperate darkness was not entirely black. I had an elementary plan for my behavior that gave me purpose and focus. I felt a small change in me starting to take shape.

The second phase of this growth took off after another conversation with my friend in which she suggested that I try to go to a place of no expectation. This hit me immediately as true and necessary—that in my interactions, I could begin to release Mr. H from any of my expectations. She said that I had the right to ask for anything I wanted, but that I should attempt to expect nothing in return. To get started, I released him from even the most basic expectations that a family member could reasonably have. I stopped expecting that he live with us, show up for dinner, or help me with the kids in any way. I also stopped having the larger expectations that were crippling me, like the expectation that he talk to me, listen to me, commit to me, or be grateful for me. It was in noticing, and then releasing, these expectations over time that I found I could encounter myself, Mr. H, and my possibilities for growth with real freedom. I learned that we start to notice what people are giving us when we drop our expectations of them.

Disclaimer: lowering your expectations of someone you are committed to is *the hardest thing ever*. I write this having achieved a moderate amount of success in this arena, but I lived it in a grueling "one step forward two steps back" manner for years. It is ingrained in us to have expectations. It is ingrained in us to be disappointed when they are not met. It is *not* ingrained in us to evaluate our expectations and discuss with our partner whether or not they are even realistic.

The first thing I noticed when I dropped my expectations was that I could actually handle my own life. I saw just how many expectations I had. And I saw how unchecked I was in them previously. As I watched familiar expectations come up minute-by-minute, I could see what a burden I put on Mr. H to be so much more than he could be, and I saw how (in that arrangement) he could never measure up to what I needed. Sure, he cleaned up the dishes after dinner, but did he see the laundry piles? Yes, he played with the kids, but did he see the house was a mess? Yes, he made money for us, but could he be less distracted? It was always a "yes, but" monologue in my head. No matter what he gave, I only saw what he didn't give. On certain days, I was mentally bombarded with the expectations I had. They kept hitting me over and over, and I started to wonder how he was able to live with me at all. He could never do right by me! I was ashamed.

I knew when we had kids that I wanted to stay home and mother them early on without outside work competing for my energy. Mr. H wanted to make his mark in his career and provide for us. We consented to this arrangement, and I think we would both do so again. It was easy with his work to see a clear boundary of responsibility. I wasn't needed to be an active participant in getting his work life done. When it came to my work, and our work, of raising the kids, it got a little more slippery. The fact that these were *our* kids gave me the illusion that everything about their care was *our* job. This blurry line was rife with my resentment. I mentally blamed him for not putting in an equal share, even though we had agreed to our roles early on. What I slipped into was the dangerous belief that unless his interest, time, and level of exhaustion matched mine, he wasn't helping. This wasn't fair.

I experimented with swinging full tilt the other way. I lived as though I would take 100% responsibility for our kids. It was a fascinating trial, and I realized that I was a competent woman and mother. I learned I could take care of our home, our kids, and our lives without him. And by releasing him from the expectation to participate in any of that, I found my own strength. This didn't stop him from participating in the way he always had, it simply shifted my reliance on him and greatly reduced my resentment toward him. I wasn't offering to care for my children at 50% effort and wondering what his contribution would look like. I offered 100%, and this new spot made me realize that I could welcome his support and not demand it.

I learned that I had become hooked into Mr. H for my whole married life. The conception that all of my burdens were his burdens was a conception that was no longer true. As a young wife, I had never stood on my own. It was always a push to make an "us." But when I grew to let go of the "us" that I thought I wanted to exist in our daily tasks, I was able to become grateful for the "us" that existed in another realm.

This gratefulness started small. I was grateful that he still slept in our home. Grateful that he was generous with money toward us, ate dinner with us, did some dishes, and played with the kids. The expectations receded. The small things suddenly became bigger. Whatever little or big actions he took were a new surprise and a blessing, not an expectation fulfilled. It made me feel, again, like a small step was being taken in the right direction. I could see him and what he was offering, not overlook him and diminish the goodness he brought to our family.

And while this effort to really start digging in on the parts of the situation that were within my control gave me purpose and determination to not let this marriage go, it was getting harder overall. The nights got quieter. Our marriage felt more strained. The reality that I was living with someone who no longer felt connected to me was wearing. No matter how much light I was pushing into the situation with my efforts to change, I felt the dark kept making its way in.

So why did I bother to keep looking for answers? Something pulled at me. I had a determined spirit to make sense of this, to get to the root of the problem, and to pull us back from the tailspin. I was convinced that my efforts mattered, and my rally would be noticed. What I didn't know was just how hard it was going to be.

QUESTIONS FOR YOUR DEEPENING

1. Where are you catastrophizing? Where are you minimizing?
2. What expectations do you have of your former partner that need recalibration?
3. You have tremendous capacity. Where are you convincing yourself that you don't?

Chapter 2

The Present Moment
(And Other Places You Don't
Want to Be)

Couples therapy. It's what everyone thinks you ought to do when the marital road gets a little bumpy. Get a neutral mediator to hear your stories, give you a few tips, and get you back out on the road. It would be awesome if it worked that way. The problem is that what most people really want, and definitely what I wanted at this point in our story, is to pay someone to talk some sense into their spouse. Make him stop! Make him go! Make her see how ridiculous she is! We go in *saying* we want to work on it, but in reality, we want someone to tell our spouse to start working harder. Because we are not the problem, they are! Surely this person, for the low cost of $150 an hour, will call my spouse to account for the ways he or she is making this marriage difficult.

In my case, the therapist was well-reputed and worked with other couples connected to our community at the time. As I drove to the first visit, I was eager to get his input. When I arrived, he terrified me. First of all, he was divorced. And not just divorced once but divorced THREE TIMES. Really? I thought to myself that maybe he should come to me for advice instead. Added to these thoughts was the fact that his appearance was slightly intimidating, and, with his background, it seemed he was not going to work with us in a traditional way. My major memory of our early visits with him was his constant insistence that we both come back to the present moment.

The present moment was an entirely new concept to me in those days. I was the kid who won the teacher's award in 6th grade for "most likely to plan out her lunches a year in advance." At this point in my story, I was a very future-focused person. I thought that the "present moment" existed for making sure the next moment was planned and supplied. If we stayed too long in a moment, who would handle dinner and get more toilet paper?

You can't go to any popular retailer now without finding some graphic tee touting how much we should all live in the moment. But in 2012, this was not yet a mainstream idea. In my heart, I felt fairly conscious of the moment, but I could tell that the therapist was looking for something a little deeper. I got a book recommendation from him on the topic and we left. Not the result I was hoping to get. And of course, with therapy, it would be another week or two before the next meeting, so I was back to being on my own trying to be in the mysterious "moment" alone.

Newsflash: when your marriage is in trouble, "the moment" sucks. The moment is unbearable. The moment is realizing your husband may not love you in the same way, and now it's time for the school fall festival. The moment is realizing everything in you feels fragile, and now you have a vacation planned with another family where your new way of relating as a troubled couple will be on total display for a week. The moment is feeling despondent, but it's time to spend the weekend at your in-laws' home. The moment is feeling like you are going to die inside,

The Present Moment (And Other Places You Don't Want to Be)

and now you need to go to the work holiday party. The moment, when you are in a potentially marriage-ending window of your life, is the only thing you don't want to be in.

Right now, while you are living in your thoroughly crappy moment, please be aware that you are not alone. In my opinion, the saddest part of divorce is not the announcement that goes out to your friends and family about the fact of your divorce. It is the deeply painful solitary slog that happens in the months and years leading up the end. These are the moments you can only share with the closest of friends or a stranger at the bar that you will never see again. What makes them so hard is the fact of their privacy. When a loved one is dying, and your community knows, the sympathy levels ride high. Grace for your unavailability, exhaustion, and general inability to hold it together abounds. But for the lead up to divorce, there is little grace. Not because it wouldn't be handed out generously by others, but because we simply cannot afford to tell everyone what is going on, especially when kids are involved.

Back to the moment. The moment—before you have the courage to really face it—can be a panicked, dead, hollow, hysterical, wild, still, volatile, frightening place. It doesn't take much effort to avoid the moment. The moment has a stench to it that no one would want to approach. You'll get to it though. The fact that you picked up this book means you have some small desire to get to it. But if you are anything like me, it is going to take some time to become courageous enough to face it.

SOMETHING BLOCKS US

You see, there are a lot of armed guards standing around the moment for you. These guards are tough. They do a very good job of keeping you from entering the moment. And they are all branded with a word, or a demand, or a disposition. And you will take each one of them on at various times during your divorce and divorce recovery process, battling them in what you think is the fight of your life.

Please know that it is the job of the guards to convince you that your true home is outside of the moment. The guards want you to believe that the battle with them is the only real battle you need to wage. They make you think that if you can count all of the guards, list out their identities, convince everyone around you of what you see, then you will finally be at peace. The guards want you to think that overcoming them in the loudest way, truly taking them down, is the only way to beat this divorce pain and win.

The guards are tricky. There are just a few when you first look, but they multiply quickly. They split from themselves into even finer distinctions of negative thought. They take turns leading the battalion. One leads the pack and exhausts you for weeks, then another picks up right where that one left off. They are also good at cloning themselves. You can talk to anyone who is going through or has approached an unwanted divorce and compare guards. They report to duty almost immediately.

Who are the guards? They wear their name tags proudly:

This is so unfair.

I'm not the kind of person who gets divorced.

Every marriage struggles, so why is mine the one that might fall apart?

We took vows. How can the vows be optional now?

How the heck did this happen?

Why is he just now speaking up?

I don't know anyone divorced that I can talk to.

The Present Moment (And Other Places You Don't Want to Be)

I'm not perfect, but she has no clue how much she has contributed to this situation.

Is he really doing this?

I need to lose weight.

I need to stop stress eating.

If I don't work out, I'll lose it.

I couldn't possibly work out today.

I'm not going to make it.

I'm always going to be this sad.

I'm unlovable.

I'm incapable of change.

I'll find another man in a minute.

No one will ever love me again.

She doesn't even work on making this better.

He's giving up too early.

I never needed him.

Wait, I totally need him!

I'm so out of here.

I'm not going anywhere; she has to own this.

I can't stop crying.

He needs to deal with his past.

She's a liar.

He's a narcissist.

She has no idea how much I do for this family.

He is terrible with money.

She needs medication.

The Best Worst Time of Your Life

Do I need medication?

He drinks too much.

I do too.

But I wouldn't have to if he would just say he is sorry.

She never sees it from my perspective.

Did he ever really love me?

She's so angry.

I'm so angry.

He's probably seeing someone.

Wait, he actually is seeing someone.

I'll kill her.

She'll replace me.

I hate her.

I hate him.

I'll kill him.

If he just would die of natural causes.

Our kids will go off the deep end.

How can she love our kids if she is willing to walk away from me and make their lives harder?

The kids will want to live with him because he's lenient.

What will I do about money?

I may need to go back to school.

I never should have limited my career.

This would actually get somewhere if she would just agree that we are going to stay together.

Most people battle with, and against, the guards from the first indication of marital tension and keep it up long after their divorce is finalized. Divorced people who only focus on the guards and ruminate on them in a repetitive, spiraling manner are marked by their refusal to align with reality. They start out stunned and end up stunted.

But the most important thing to know about the guards is that they are animated only by you and me. We are the puppet masters. When we don't pick up a sword against them, they simply lie on the ground. They don't run off and they don't disappear, they just exist as powerless figures. And when they lie there powerlessly, it is possible to tiptoe into the moment that they were guarding without any resistance.

Then what happens? If you can stop with the guards, you can start with yourself.

YOUR BRAIN ON DIVORCE

Brain science supports this understanding. You see, there are essentially three parts to your brain: the reptilian brain, the mammalian brain, and the neocortex brain. There are fancier words that neurologists would use, but let's keep it simple. They work in concert doing a number of functions that play out in the daily life of a divorcing person.

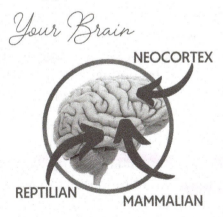

Your divorce will have you firmly lodged in reptilian brain right out of the gate. Your reptilian brain is where all of these guards live and craft their plan to keep you scared and reactive and blaming. The reptilian brain does its job like it's Employee of the Month. The reptilian brain is where your fight or flight response largely lives. It feeds on fear. It's preoccupied with aggression and territory, and it gets pretty obsessive. It's a super useful part of our brain in certain situations, but in divorce, it can get drunk on possibilities and squash any efforts you were trying to make toward being calm or amicable. The reptilian brain is in there saying "Be proud of me! You haven't died! I'll defend you to the end!" It's busy being instinctual and caring almost exclusively about your survival. It's part caveman, part sneaky marketer, and it plays on the part of you that is freaked out. It sees many things as threats. It is naturally resistant.

While the reptilian brain is working overtime to not let you die from divorce, it cannot and will not care about your other noble goals in life besides survival. It won't support you in your effort to develop healthy communication skills with your divorcing spouse. It won't remind you that your better self wanted to keep your voice at a pleasant tone when you got triggered by another last-minute parenting schedule change. It won't elevate your game. It cares about keeping you alive. It doesn't care about you becoming your best self. It won't advise you to stop Googling "am I ok?" each night.

Also, as a free party prize, when the reptilian brain leads the way, it leaves a physical mark on you. When it has been operating at high speed, you will be mentally and physically exhausted. Fight or flight is draining. We were meant to activate it when a real threat presents itself, but divorce can make us lay down roots in fight or flight. Given that most divorces can take years to walk

30

The Present Moment (And Other Places You Don't Want to Be)

through, let alone heal from, your reptilian brain living can take a tremendous amount of energy from you.

When you get that notification on your phone and you see that it's from your former spouse? That feeling you get—it's your reptilian brain running the show. You feel scared, threatened, on defense, not sure, wondering what is going to show up. Even if the text is just "Mia wanted you to know she got an A on her spelling test", your reptilian brain went on the defensive before you read it. Because this person you were married to, who you were aligned with and on the same team with for a short or long period, you now perceive as being against you. How could you not? The divorce papers themselves typically say His Last Name versus Your Last Name. It's laid out as a fight in the very language the system employs.

Your reptilian brain is committed to preserving you. It's the part of your brain that feels threatened by a loss of control, especially as you walk into an unknown legal system to handle your divorce. It's threatened by a sense of urgency, and it gets loud when it thinks a decision has to be made quickly. It's threatened by what might happen to your access to, or your time with your children, and it barks orders to hold on to what you think is yours. It's the part that squashes your self-esteem when you contemplate how it would feel to take the clothes off the body you have and offer yourself again to a new person. And it's deeply threatened at the thought of what your finances will and will not look like a couple years from now.

You can see how the reptilian brain is to blame for the mental nightmare and physical fatigue you are currently carrying. If you keep letting it run the show, it will keep you from everything the better part of yourself imagines for you.

31

Before I meet with a coaching client, they complete a worksheet so I can get a glance at what struggles they are going through. One of the questions in that worksheet asks, "If the biggest struggle you were going through in your divorce was resolved or if you felt you were handling it well, what would your life look like?" Without exception, an element of their answer always includes some variation on the theme of "I would be at peace." They write about how they would sleep better, communicate without anger, obsess less, and focus more. They say they would be less triggered, more relaxed, less defeated, and more boundaried.

These beautiful and totally attainable goals are not available when you lead with the reptilian brain. The reptilian brain can't even imagine these evolved, self-loving, or peaceful scenarios. It's too busy pedaling so hard to make sure you get what is yours and monitor every threat to your wellbeing. My divorce coaching is designed to acknowledge, define, and create awareness around what triggers your reptilian brain into action. We explore what buttons of yours get pushed (and by whom) that can unleash this beast to go into overdrive. Once we can see and know them, we can start to consider leading with the neocortex instead.

The neocortex part of your brain is beautiful. She is the higher order part of your brain. Responsible for language and sensory motor processing, she is more careful and deliberate than the reptilian brain. Where the reptilian brain loves "Fight or Flight," the neocortex loves, as Kelly McGonigal coined it, the "Pause and Plan" strategy. It's less reactive, more thoughtful, and truly the better part of yourself. Where the reptilian brain wants to protect you, the neocortex already knows you are safe and seeks to build an even better sense of comfort in your unpredictable surroundings.

The Present Moment (And Other Places You Don't Want to Be)

It's the part of your brain that can feel apprehensive as you walk into an unknown legal system, but also reassured that you have figured out hard things before and know how to ask good questions. When it thinks a decision has to be made quickly, it steps up to suggest taking 24 hours and seeing what comes up. During conversations around your access to or your time with your children, it gets you in that genuine love space to consider what is truly best for your children—even if it's hard for you. When you contemplate what it looks like to take the clothes off the body you have and offer it again to a new person, it comes alongside you and knows there is a person who will love you just as you are. And when future finances are considered, it makes a game plan based on solid evidence.

Do you see how much *easier* it is to think about divorce from the perspective of the neocortex? Wouldn't everyone want to live from this free, comforted, reassured, confident, flexible space? Of course they would, but few do. Why?

When the reptilian brain gets triggered, your brain is literally hijacked for between 5 and 15 minutes. In that space, access to the neocortex is significantly, if not entirely, blocked. Blocked. You couldn't get to it even if you wanted it, and I know you want it! If that's the case, how could we ever get to a place where we don't get hijacked so frequently?

We practice. It's a practice. Rolling out the red carpet for your neocortex is the single most important step you can take to change the tone and your experience of your divorce. With practice, you learn what triggers you and you learn to pause and plan. This is easier said than done, but entirely doable with practice. And that is what the practices in this book are designed to introduce you to.

I have a solid list of known triggers in my life with Mr. H. I get triggered by less than exact trade off times. By texts or emails that go more than 24 hours without acknowledgement. By how we hear and don't hear each other. Earlier on I was triggered by almost every single point of connection we had. Every one of them caused a reptilian hijacking scenario: his tone, his presence, his absence, his comments, his mannerisms. Everything he did created that threatened, wigged out, and over time, dangerous life-sucking response. And, of course, it had nothing to do with him. He still has the same tone, presence, absence, comments, and mannerisms. They don't bother me now, just like they don't really bother anyone else. It has taken several years to develop the skills I need to enjoy a much shorter list and a much more expansive heart from which to respond to the relatively small list of triggers that remains.

How did I get there? By quieting myself over, and over, and over again. I trained myself to get out of the reptilian brain attack. This was a near-impossible task at first. My response felt uncontrollable. I was at the mercy of it, and in most cases, it felt like the situation warranted a high-energy response. I had to learn the hard and slow way that my hysterics weren't actually warranted. The triggers got at me because that's what naturally happens when you get in a divorce. It wasn't the only way to live. It felt like it was. I had to take a different approach.

YOUR GO-TO PRACTICE

Remember the guards? Those reptilian brain soldiers that send up the alarm and call to arms? The next time you get an experience of one, I want you to slow down and not react. If you can just get to and do this part—slowing down and not reacting—you win. If you can take it another step, below are some questions that can help you sit in the post-guards moment with purpose

34

The Present Moment (And Other Places You Don't Want to Be)

and direction. I started visiting these questions as regularly as possible shortly after my snowy walk where I thought I would die of heartbreak. I still work with them today to keep myself and my reptilian brain in check.

1. What am I scared of or anxious about?

    This question is about acknowledging that almost every negative emotion going on in your relational struggles comes back to fear. It feels like anger ("How in the world is he getting away with this?!") but its essence is really fear ("What does my life look like when he actually gets away with this?"). Remember, fear will accompany you on this journey. It only becomes an enemy when it stays in the shadows. Use this question to pull it into the light.

    This question slows down the reptilian brain and starts to create some distance between you and the situation itself. You lovingly draw near to yourself and just inquire a simple question and listen for the answer. It's ok to be scared. It's ok to be anxious. Just get specific on it. Science has shown us that our calmer thinking brain gets engaged when we write things down. Get a pen and write your answers down. What are you really afraid of in this particular situation?

2. How can I self soothe?

    Self-soothing is typically associated with sleep training in babies. Babies who master self-soothing can fall asleep on their own and don't need an adult to step in and reassure, touch, rock, or guide them back to sleep. As adults, particularly adults handling large uncomfortable transitional moments in their lives, we need to explore what it means to self-soothe too. While we don't usually need to self-soothe to get to sleep, we do need to self-soothe to help us exit the wild, loud noise of our reptilian minds and enter the deeper heart center.

35

How you pursue self-soothing initially can look like a number of healthy and unhealthy responses. You may believe you are self-soothing by drinking, talking incessantly about the situation, eating, shopping, or getting lost in your phone. This is, in actuality, more buffering than self-soothing. Buffering puts distance between you and your real feelings. In the case of drinking, it turns down the voices in your head that are in overdrive with negative thoughts. Buffering doesn't cause you to feel, address, and work with these thoughts to create a different reality. It delays the fact that what you were dealing with before you started drinking will be there afterwards as well. Buffering behaviors dull and delay often with negative longer-term consequences. Self-soothing activities feel on purpose, provide true comfort, and contribute to positive consequences. Self-soothing might include doing something like journaling, taking a walk or hike, meditating, reading, or doing yoga. It might also look like sitting quietly and feeling the pain, fear, and darkness. It asks the question, what can I do right now to introduce calm to this situation that will still have a payoff for me 24 hours from now?

3. What do I need to confront in my myself?

Confronting yourself simply means the ability to see your faults/growth areas/patterns, seek to be responsible for them, and commit to exposing the truth about them. What it does not mean is seeing your faults/growth areas/patterns and shaming and berating yourself. Compassionate self-confrontation is done out of a desire to become a better person and a desire to develop an honest relationship with yourself and your reality.

It asks, "What truths in my own development and growth are bringing this issue to a fevered pitch for me right now?

The Present Moment (And Other Places You Don't Want to Be)

Which limitations of my own are making it difficult for me to have healthy reactions to this situation? When done well, after you confront yourself and see the truth of yourself, you will likely think, "Yeah, that makes sense. I get why this is still so hard for me. I'm still growing in my ability to _____." Confronting ourselves deepens our self-awareness and identifies self-imposed barriers.

4. How do I contribute to my own unhappiness?

In the darkness of divorce days, for some reason, we love to make sure we go the extra mile to keep the curtains closed as well. I did it too. It's dark, let's make it darker. It's really sadistic to do this to ourselves, but we persist. Exploring how you contribute to your own unhappiness is the chance to shine a very small spotlight on those things over which you might actually have some influence: most notably, your thoughts.

You can contribute to your own unhappiness in so many ways that you could probably write them into a separate book. Ruminating, the obsessive retelling of events to yourself and others, is a favorite way. Another way that people contribute to their unhappiness is by expecting things to be different than they are. This can look like impatience, catastrophizing, and resistance. One of the hardest parts of divorce recovery is how long it can take before you realize that your former partner is not the singular cause of your unhappiness. You are a key player too. See what roadblocks you're putting in your own way on this step.

5. What is true today about me no matter what?

Remembering what is true about you is vital to your survival. The narrative you tell yourself has the power to shape your final destination, and it must be shepherded regularly to end up where you hope to be. While your routine, your address, and even your name may change through this process, there are things about you that will not change. Don't forget them.

You might remember that you are deeply loved by the divine, that you give 100% to your kids, or that you've made it through so much and have the power to make it through more. It may be a more feeble truth, and that's ok. My friend Miryam loves to say, "You have a 100% track record of getting through the day." As you nurture this practice over time, my hope is that you will deepen in your ability to affirm the profound strength of heart that dwells in you. It is this part that will keep you moving forward.

I'll give you a picture of how this reflective framework worked in my own life as I divorced. My sticking point was the idea that having my kids less than 100% of the time was going to irreparably damage my life and my relationship with them. As soon as I started having those thoughts, the guards reported to duty:

The kids won't love me as much as they do him.

They'll like the pool better at dad's house.

He's more fun; they won't want to see me as often.

I might miss big events in their lives when they are with him.

I'll get left out of something amazing they do just with him.

I'll not be a mom if they aren't here getting mothered.

The Present Moment (And Other Places You Don't Want to Be)

I then tried to engage my neocortex by submitting this struggle to the five questions.

1. What am I scared of or anxious about?

    I'm petrified that I will not see my kids enough, and we will have a difficult relationship going forward. They will be distant from me and not have their mom around for all of the important moments. I won't know how to parent them when they are away from me.

2. How can I self soothe?

    Buffering would pick a night of drinking wine. Self-soothing would not. Self-soothing has two important distinctions—it deals with real feelings and it has positive consequences for me for at least 24 hours afterward. I am going to experiment with sitting still and mentally meditating on the word "safe" for the next 2 minutes and see what comes up. I am going to do this because my anxiety about this issue makes me feel very unsafe and insecure in my future, and meditating brings me out of my reptilian brain and into my neocortex.

3. What do I need to confront in my myself?

    When I look at myself in this situation, with these thoughts, I need to confront that I fear the love my kids and I share is not strong enough to weather these changes. I need to confront that I see myself as powerless in my relationship with them; I'm a victim of the situation. I also need to confront that I'm not remembering how much control I have over how I conduct myself with them and how I build that relationship day by day regardless of our circumstances. I can confront that I work hard at being a connected mother, and that I can read, study, and ask questions of others about how I will maintain that connection when we are not together.

The Best Worst Time of Your Life

4.   How do I contribute to my own unhappiness?

I contribute to my own unhappiness by choosing to believe that my relationship with my kids is deeply threatened by these changes and has little chance of surviving well. I am adding catastrophizing. Yes, the worst thing *could* happen: I could be estranged from my kids. But, also, the *best* thing could happen: I could invest in making meaningful healthy connections with them wherever they are in the world. I'm also making myself unhappy by acting like I have no power to influence the situation. I'm not giving my kids enough credit for just how much they love me. I'm not trusting the divine to grow a love in us that is unbreakable.

5.   What is true today about me no matter what?

What is true about me today is that I love my kids. I love them enough to be afraid about what our future relationship will look like. I also know that what is true about me is that I will work very hard during these hard times to make sure my relationship with my kids stays strong. I am a fighter. I am a learner. I am willing to move into unknown spaces and build new realities. I have friends that support me in this effort. I am not a quitter.

So, you see, what started with high anxiety and high fear and high reptilian brain activity was slowly walked down a path with these questions into a much calmer and truer spot. Our initial high alert reactions disguise themselves as absolute truth, and when we bring them into the light and really tip them over and examine them from all angles, they are really not so true. They are waypoints. A waypoint is simply a point of reference to help you know where you are. It is not a destination. It gets you closer to it.

The Present Moment (And Other Places You Don't Want to Be)

If we can welcome these wild, crazy, and scary thoughts and walk with them through this framework of examination, we can find that rested and possible spot within ourselves that knows we actually *can* make it through this. It actually *will* be ok.

During my darkest days, I used to ask my friend Amie Jo all the time, "Is it going to be OK?" I did this so often that she bought me a framed print for my home with the words "It's going to be OK." I had to borrow her confidence for a while. I would call my friend Sheila and say, "Just tell me it's going to be OK," and she would assure me it would. Several years into my divorce healing, I called her with that same plea, and she said, "I think you can tell yourself that now." And she was right. You may need to borrow someone's reassurance and confidence along the way as well, but know that it's a waypoint too. This practice of questioning your own fears and anxieties will help you develop the ability to say it to yourself. After a while, what you know to be true about yourself will be the starting point of how you approach these tricky spots.

You can put every thought to the test in this way. Your finances, your living situation, and your parenting time are just a few examples. These questions are your entry point. They will be answered over and over again with different starting topics each time. You may roll your eyes at just how often you need to submit to this examination, but you will never regret the investment in your heart that these questions make possible.

Let's get back to therapy before we move on. The initial driving force that gets you to therapy is rarely the agenda you stick to after the first meeting. For me, it felt like we were discussing Mr. H's impending loss of his job, his inability to express his dissatisfaction about our relationship, and my wondering when he would get back to normal. The time in therapy didn't bend to what I thought it needed to be to get us

41

The Best Worst Time of Your Life

back on track. Therapy can feel like that. It takes the mess you know you are in and puts it in front of a warped mirror. You can walk out of a session feeling so buoyed and full of hope and find out from your spouse in the debrief later that night that they felt marginalized and not heard. WHAT??!! Therapy becomes this beacon where you think you will get things straightened out, but certain nights it can feel like it is only twisting them more.

It's still worth it. Don't quit on therapy. But do consider quitting on the posture you have when you go in each time. If your posture is hopeful that your spouse will finally understand you, follow through on what was agreed upon last time, or finally admit to something, you're wasting the money you are spending. You can't go in with that posture and get what you want. Therapy, done well, and at this stage, is a safe space to experiment with making space for your spouse's reality. Ouch, I know.

You likely have already developed an allergy to your spouse's reality. To you that reality may be made of fake news, but to your spouse, it is everything. You don't need to change your partner's reality. You don't need to "believe" in it. You don't need to change yours either. What you *do* need to do is make room for the reality that your partner brings. Make room. Don't defend. Don't dispute. Allow. Dive into their reality like an embedded reporter in a war zone. Flesh it out, turn it over, and see it. Witness it. You don't need to prove anything. When you spend your time proving, you will leave the therapist's office once again wondering if it was worth it. When you spend your time exploring, looking directly at your partner's foreign reality, you may actually get somewhere. And if nothing else, you have given the gift you most long to receive yourself: the acknowledgement that your experience of your life together and potentially apart is worth noticing. When we practice allowing other people their truth, we move that much closer to our coveted destination: acceptance.

42

I know that you didn't want this divorce, even if you're the one who ultimately does ask for it. No one gets married and hopes that everything will fall apart. But it is good to look around and see where you sit now. What you never dreamed of is now your day-to-day life. If you can make space, you may find that while you did not ask for it, your life was begging for it. I can hear the brakes in your brain pushing back on that suggestion, and I will leave you there for the moment in your reptilian brain to resist it.

QUESTIONS FOR YOUR DEEPENING

1. What are the top 3 guards that you war with?

2. Choose one guard and walk through the five questions with it:

   What am I scared of or anxious about?
   How can I self-soothe?
   What do I need to confront in myself?
   How do I contribute to my own unhappiness?
   What is true today about me no matter what?

   Is there anything appealing about approaching that guard from your thoughtful brain instead of your fight or flight brain?

3. Where in your day or week could you set aside time to commit to thoughtful processing of the most pressing guard?

Chapter 3

You Need A New Triangle

I read celebrity divorce announcements with raised eyebrows. Alright, I actually read them and then typically start in on how contrived they sound. They have such glowing language about how they are planning a beautiful separation and side-by-side child rearing. "We've made the mutual decision to no longer continue this journey as married partners but continue as partners in raising our beautiful children." Or, "We have reached the end of this chapter and we wish each other the best." Then they go on as to how they would prefer some privacy, a request which the American media will of course not be able to honor. We love a good tragedy, especially when it's not ours.

These announcements are the ultimate in public relations, I know. I get why they are doing this. They have careers built on personas, and they want to keep them intact. They need to time them between their creative pursuits. I also think on some level that they also truly believe what they (or their staff) wrote. They do, in fact, have aspirations to part well. I respect that.

But these glowing announcements leave the rest of us who find ourselves divorcing in a troubled space. Just like their celebrity lives, which we think run smoothly due to housekeepers, chefs, nannies, and drivers, we believe that even their divorces are admirable. Their satin hair and perfect skin are photographed next to those shiny divorce announcements and we start to think, "Why can't I do it like them? Why can't my divorce be more dignified, less bothered, and tied up neatly?"

This trend toward the soaring language of glossy divorces is driven largely by the introduction of social media into the mainstream. In the 1970s, people didn't go carbon copy a joint divorce letter to distribute to their friends to dissect. They told the people they wanted to tell as they saw them, the rest was spread through gossip. It was a reality, but it wasn't often written. It didn't get edited. It didn't have a particular tone.

But with the advent of social media, our messages reach wider audiences, and the words matter in a different way. Divorce announcements are simply another way to control someone's image and appearance. What does that do for those of us going through a divorce without a public relations team? Quite simply, it reinforces our failure. These public announcements set up a false standard that very few of us (even the original couple) can meet, and they leave us struggling to try to measure up.

I honestly don't think people are lying when they write these. I wouldn't accuse you of lying if you wrote one either. I think like most online postings, they are aspirational. And there is a layer of that aspiration that I want to underscore as very useful. Casting forth a vision that says, "We are trying to do this well, we are trying to love our children through a crappy time, and we would love your support" is beautiful. You should definitely say this. You should definitely believe it.

My push back against these announcements is not that we shouldn't issue them, it's just that they are profoundly incomplete.

Seven years after the finalizing of my own divorce, I can tell you that I can write a beautiful uncoupling statement with a pure, real, lived life behind it to support it. "We are trying to do this well, we are trying to love our children through a time of rearrangement in our family, and we would love your support." At first, while that sentence was still true, it also had another sentence before it. "I am so terribly ruined by this whole situation, barely able to cope, failing in most of my responsibilities, deeply ashamed, scared to death of what is happening to my kids, terrified of my shaky finances, uncertain of the road ahead, surprised by my unhealthy survival tactics, angry beyond measure at my soon-to-be former partner, and desperately wanting all of these hard times to be over." That's the sentence that gets left out. That's the sentiment that gets lost next to the pretty smiles and idealized statements about a great partnership in the future. So, in addition to living through the failure that feel, we also look around us and pile on the shame for not looking and feeling more polished and optimistic.

"DO BETTER AND BE BETTER" DOESN'T WORK

You'll get a lot of "do better and be better" messages from well-meaning people in your life who read these celebrity announcements and think they are an example of how it can be done well. Anticipate a few of these well-intentioned remarks from your friends:

I hope you can take the high road. It's so lovely when people tell you to take the high road in your great uncoupling. That was really adorable advice for me in the beginning. When it is given to you as you are starting out, feel free to smile, nod, and then disregard it. When you are first confronting the idea of a divorce you didn't ask for, I give you total permission to yell at the top of your lungs, "Screw the high road!" Truly. Screw it. You can't will yourself there at the beginning. You will get there with some work. But it's just. So. High. And right now, you're low. You're so low. Frankly, it's really important to travel every last mile of the low road before you even begin to contemplate the high road. There are a lot of really great scenic views, dirt trails, and breakdowns you need to experience on the low road to appreciate just how high you are when you arrive at that most glorious destination of the high road.

You just need to forgive and move on. This is also a common refrain from the cheap seats. "You just need to forgive and move on." That word "just" is almost as defeating as "forgive." As if we "just" wake up and "just" decide to "just" forgive. It doesn't happen like that. Don't even try to make it happen like that. The forgiveness that you think you give under this kind of pressure is made out of vapor and will disappear. You will likely need to strain toward, wrestle with, and fight for forgiveness over a long period of time. It's not easy. The process is hard, but your efforts at marching toward it will change you in ways you will treasure.

Put the kids first. Again, you agree with this. Unfortunately, hidden in this statement is the idea that you might not put them first. It also presumes that if you do the good work of putting your children first, you won't run into any troubles with your divorce. This is not true, and it is harmful for your recovery. Married people are told to put their relationship first ahead of the kids. The minute you get divorced, you are told to switch that. Plenty of married couples disagree on what is best for their children. As divorcing parents, you should anticipate this will continue. What does putting the kids first mean anyway? The kids get what they want? It is a complex task to put the kids first. Sometimes putting the kids first means mom needs a break to regroup. Sometimes it means dad is on a call to make money to put your kid in basketball camp. What "first" means is tricky at best and not a great metric for how you make it through this process.

I never liked your spouse anyway. Ouch. This one can hurt even as you might like to hear it too. Unfortunately, it has the back-end effect of causing you to question the nature of the relationship that you and your former spouse had with that friend. People who are accustomed to the combative American divorce system immediately seek to take a side and demonize the other. They mean well, but it can hurt.

I have a great lawyer if you need one. This one is a mixed bag too. On the one hand, you hear the word divorce and you automatically think you need a lawyer. On the other hand, you may be someone who wants to try to go it alone. Either way, the offer of a lawyer in the case of divorce is often premature. When you find out you are getting divorced, your threat level goes through the roof. You want some version of a bouncer to ward off these threats, and the lawyer gets called instead. I cannot emphasize enough that the life you want five years from now with your former spouse should dictate whether, when, and what type of lawyer you call. You rarely need to start with a lawyer. The friend that offers the lawyer may actually have the best lawyer for you, but there is an introspective process before that call that will bear heavily on your outcomes.

You'll totally find love and get married again. It feels so good to be told you're pretty or you're a catch, especially when you've been rejected by your former spouse. But most divorcing people are convinced the risk of pain and hurt does not outweigh the possibility of new love. You also don't usually have the bandwidth to be in a relationship when you are working through the layers and layers of untangling from the relationship you are in right now. In addition, putting yourself back into the dating scene is daunting at any age. You might find love again, but it's not the time to think about it now.

You'll feel better, it will just take time. Time is that thing that you want to fast forward right about now. Time drags on and drags you down and is making you miserable. It takes time to talk about the failing marriage with each other. To talk about it with a therapist. To sort out the impact of finances. To talk about it with your kids. It takes time for the lawyers to get the paperwork filed. Then there is time for the waiting period to pass before it's final. Time feels slow on a long weekend until your kids come back to your home. You will need time until you just feel better. You've seen time work in your past, but this is bigger than anything you've ever faced. What if time met its match in your divorce?

My Grandma Kuhns had a saying, "The hardest thing about time is that time takes time." Isn't that the truth? Time does happen to be your one ally in this miserable mess, in that it never stops moving forward. Every day it marches on. And some well-wishers may even try to encourage you with that familiar phrase "Time heals all wounds." There is certainly some truth to that. Again, it's incomplete. I might rephrase it to say "time *put to your good use* heals *many* of your wounds."

All of these comments come from good places in the people that say them to you. Just because a friend makes one of these remarks isn't grounds for dismissing them. But you may benefit from knowing why they say them. Your friends are extremely uncomfortable with your divorce and the pain that you are in as a result of it. They want you to be happy. They want you to feel better. They want you to feel they are on your side. They want you to be hopeful. And you know what? With intention to the process described later in this book, you probably will be those things again.

50

But if you are anything like me, it will be a long and winding process. The Stages of Grief developed by Elizabeth Kubler-Ross and popularized in her book *On Death and Dying* published in 1969 hint at the initial stages of the process. The Stages of Grief were originally proposed by Kubler-Ross as the natural progression of reactions of terminally ill patients as they processed their approaching deaths. The Stages have since gained traction as part of what survivors of loss also experience.

The stages include Denial, Anger, Bargaining, Depression, and Acceptance. Denial encompasses that shaky time of disbelief and shock that accompanies the early days of the loss. Anger swells against any nearby party: your former partner, your parents, your God. Bargaining is that period of begging that you could just go back in time, just have one more chance to do it differently, do it better. Depression is the deep, dark, hopeless stage of grief that feels endless and all-encompassing. Acceptance emerges as we begin to align ourselves more with the reality of what life looks like going forward.

As the understanding of these stages took root in our culture in the late 1900s, they unfortunately were initially understood as a linear path. As such, people felt they were "failing" to grieve correctly and in proper order. They took too long in one stage and skipped another one entirely. Toward the end of her life, Kubler-Ross was careful to clarify that she never intended these steps to happen in order or in equal time. Just before her death, along with co-author David Kessler, Kubler-Ross went on in her book *On Grief and Grieving* to add a lesser-known sixth stage of grief: Finding Meaning. This stage is our attempt to make sense of the loss and live in a more aligned and peaceable way with it. It takes Acceptance and mines it for gold.

When we think about these six stages in relationship to divorce, and particularly coping with the fallout of divorce, the first four stages are where we spend the most time. Unfortunately, while we are circling around suffering through stages one through four, the only thing we dream about are stages five and six—Acceptance and Finding Meaning.

I dare you to find someone who has plumbed the edges of all written and spoken material in their search to find the golden ticket to acceptance more than I have. I have searched every internet browser, scoured bookstores, libraries, podcasts, public events—you name it, I've sought it out. The thing I craved most in my divorce process was to figure out acceptance. Because, in my mind, if I could just get to acceptance, then this whole mental gymnastics and difficult suffering part would be *over*. Like you, I just wanted it to be over.

I wanted it to be like it was before the divorce ever started. I wanted my mind to wander to the things it used to think about. I didn't want to keep sitting and plotting fake revenge, hashing out why I was so hurt, and figuring out how to make this part of my life look recognizable. I wanted to be free of what seemed like an ongoing, never ending PROCESS.

My Grandma Kuhns also had another zinger for me. It was often the form of a prayer for both of us: Lord, give us patience, and give it to us RIGHT NOW! We want the result. We want the end. We want the new thing to bloom. We want winter to close out and spring to show its buds. We are not good with the in-between.

Pema Chödrön, an American Buddhist nun, writes beautifully about the in-between in her *Lion's Roar* article called "Six Kinds of Loneliness." In it, she says, "As human beings, not only do we seek resolution, but we also feel that we deserve resolution.

However, not only do we not deserve resolution, we suffer from resolution. We don't deserve resolution; we deserve something better than that. We deserve our birthright, which is the middle way, an open state of mind that can relax with paradox and ambiguity...The middle way is wide open, but it's tough going, because it goes against the grain of an ancient neurotic pattern that we all share. When we feel lonely, when we feel hopeless, what we want to do is move to the right or the left. We don't want to sit and feel what we feel. We don't want to go through the detox. Yet the middle way encourages us to do just that. It encourages us to awaken the bravery that exists in everyone without exception, including you and me."

We don't deserve resolution; we suffer from it. It's a deep dive to wrap your head around this one. Not many of us find suffering in the resolution of difficult things. It's usually the opposite. The suffering seems to be a constant part of the always-changing nature of our situation. As we go back and forth (and skip over, and return) to Denial, Anger, Bargaining, and Depression again and again, our focus is not on the ways to keep our situation unresolved. We feel a primal yearning to bring them to an end. A resolution. Acceptance. Finding Meaning.

But what if Chödrön is on to something? What if there is a secret tucked in here that could lighten even a small part of the weight that you carry during this time?

Chödrön believes that there is tremendous value in the processes that can fully mature in us. Our tendency to scoot out from underneath the pressure of the tension and the unknown is universal, yet it does us no lasting good. The "middle way" she discusses highlights the liminal nature of divorce. We know we are leaving something, for some of us a beloved something, for others a despised something, and we are entering an unknown something. We yearn deeply for a definition of the new thing.

We need to know what we are leaving (marriage) and what we are going toward (as yet undefined).

SAY GOODBYE TO YOUR MARRIAGE TRIANGLE

When we think about the structure of our marriage, it's helpful to consider this image from Robert J. Sternberg, Professor of Human Development at Cornell University:

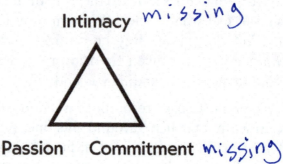

This visual describes Sternberg's Triangular Theory of Love and it understands deep, abiding love to be the healthy and balanced relationship of Intimacy, Passion, and Commitment between two people. Most marriages start with a strong rush of Passion, the physical attraction, romance, and arousal sensations that drive our coupling. The Intimacy component is defined by our general sense of liking the other person. This involves our sense of companionship, connectedness, and close bond with our partner. The final component, Commitment, is that most basic fidelity of choosing the other person as an object of your love and also choosing the long-term nature of the relationship. Sternberg is clear with Commitment that you can love a person without a commitment; similarly, you can commit to a person while not necessarily loving them.

This is what made your marriage. The rise and fall and combination of these three components created the marriage you inhabited. Over time, these elements shifted and became more and less prominent. The existence of one element or the strong combination of any two of these elements really impacted the way you perceived and experienced the relationship. Sternberg lays out 8 different types of relationships that emerge from the various combinations of Intimacy, Passion, and Commitment:

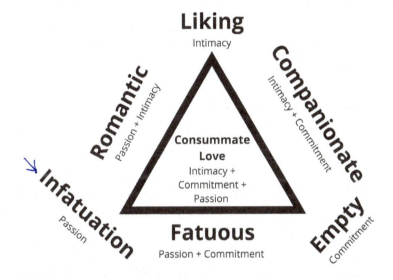

- Liking love is what you get when you have Intimacy but no Passion or Commitment.
- Infatuated love is high on Passion, but lacking Intimacy and Commitment.
- Empty love is strong on Commitment, even when there is no Passion or Intimacy.
- Romantic love promotes Intimacy and Passion, but is low on Commitment.

- Companionate love says "I love my bond with you" (Intimacy) and "I'm committed to you" (Commitment) even when there is low to no experience of Passion.

- Fatuous love is the experience of Passion and Commitment despite the lack of Intimacy.

- Consummate, or as Sternberg calls it "complete love," is produced by the expression of all three elements: Intimacy, Passion, and Commitment.

- Nonlove refers simply to the absence of all three elements of love.

For most of my clients, I observe that their marriages began with a Consummate marriage enjoying high levels of Intimacy, Passion, and Commitment. After a period of time, either Passion or Intimacy faded, and they moved into Liking or Companionate Love. They no longer felt the physical rush and chemical arousal for their partner, or they no longer really liked the person or felt the strength of bond previously in place. Whatever may have led to the diminishing of the Passion and Intimacy in their relationship, what they were left with was Commitment. Sternberg describes a Commitment-only relationship as empty, and it is this emptiness that forces one partner's hand toward divorce.

Even if your relationship followed a different path, the end result for divorcing couples is Nonlove. My divorcing friends, you know the Nonlove relationship. You've lived it. It's where you think "I'm no longer passionate about you physically, I no longer like you or feel this connected bond with you (or you don't feel it with me), and I'm not willing to move ahead with the commitment I offered you in the past (or I am but you aren't)." Nonlove stings. It's the reason the divorce process is so exquisitely painful. Here you are shedding every piece of what made you a couple, making complex and highly consequential decisions together, and figuring out how to raise your most precious children in this arrangement. Nonlove is also what leads to the traditional divorce debris wherein parents struggle to deal with their own grief and rage, kids suffer under the strain of their emotionally taxed parents, and the tensions between mom and dad remain years after the legal process is complete.

Recognize this for a moment: when the Triangle of Love is eliminated, and your marriage has shifted to Nonlove, there is no longer a structure around which to build a future relationship, especially as it relates to co-parenting. The divorce process eliminates the very arrangement around which we gathered ourselves as a couple, and now we have no place to gather. What typically happens next is we pitch a tent next to the leftovers and stare at them, throwing the former components into the weak fire we can make with them. And we stand there freezing.

To truly deepen in your divorce and pursue true wholeness and healing, we need a new triangle.

SAY HELLO TO YOUR DIVORCE TRIANGLE

Your new Divorce Triangle has the same components—Intimacy, Passion, and Commitment—but to build a post-divorce life and family, we need to shift the direction of the energy in all three.

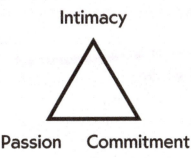

In my adapted Triangular Theory of Divorce, Intimacy is driven by the acknowledgement that finding a way to like your former partner would make the divorce and co-parenting more bearable. How do you bring that about? You start to raise into your consciousness the parts of your former partner that still serve the situation and benefit your kids. You no longer only air your grievances, but you recognize that your former partner can also bring even a small measure of goodness to your now differently-shaped family.

Passion is now in pursuit of self-growth and awareness. Most people going through and recovering from divorce are passionate about blaming their former spouse, seething about injustices, and complaining about how hard it is to bear. Start there. But what if that same passion to undo got redirected to building up? What if you could point your passion in a direction to electrify and push you deeper into what it would take to really feel good again? This kind of passion is willing to experiment, to be consistent, and to trust that openings occur when you stick with something. When you deepen your passion for self-growth, you are willing to confront yourself, not just your former spouse, and face how you could be causing your own troubles. You are also faithful to a self-soothing process that takes you off the reactive vindictive train and brings you back into a comfortable spot in yourself.

Your Commitment is no longer to the marriage relationship; it is now a commitment to engaging the post-divorce relationship with your former partner in new ways. It acknowledges that while you may get out of the marriage, as parents, you never get out of the relationship. This commitment drives you to learn your former partner's operating system and manage it in a way that no longer rocks you so much and so often. It pushes you to keep at it even when giving up feels easier and warranted.

Learn Seth's operating system.

These are the basics of your new post-divorce life structure.

I talk to many people who want this expression of life post-divorce to be true in their lives. Most of them are willing to do the work. But while we love to live from the new place of maturation, it is our perseverance during the process and the illumination we seek during that time that truly shapes the maturity we want to fully carry. It's not enough to sit idly by and hope that time will do its good work. We have to lean into the growth curve while acknowledging the in-between.

INVITE THE IN-BETWEEN

It would be easier if you could invite the in-between. Could you make a temporary but comfortable home in your in-between? That itchy scratchy place is actually your first destination in the process. Some thoughts you may want to furnish that home with:

Be gentle with yourself. This was the refrain of one of my mentors in the divorce process and it couldn't be truer. You will be hard on yourself on the regular. Keep reminding yourself that the celebrity image of pristine divorce is not reality. The reality is that your life is coming undone. It's helpful to ask ourselves how we might talk to our own friends or daughters if we found them in the same situation. Offer that same kindness to yourself.

You only have half of the story at any point in time. You don't get to tell your former partner's part of the story. You also don't have access to the new story he or she is developing now as you separate lives. You will act like you know, and you will erroneously and unfairly fill in the missing pieces. You will try to get the whole story back in your hands to save your own image but also to try to make sense of it. Some things won't make sense because you only have access to your half of the story.

Find your country music. I can hear you groan. People either love this genre or hate it. I love country music, and not just because everyone loses spouses and drowns their sorrows. I grew up in a small town in the Midwest, and this music was the only soundtrack available. When I went through my divorce recovery, I was reminded of just how much I love this music. I started going to concerts and reconnecting with what gave me so much joy. You don't need to listen to country music. But you need to be on the lookout for the activity or experience that feeds that part of you that needs something fun, life-giving, and supportive to get you through this.

These three thoughts will start to create a soft space in this new in-between home you'll occupy while you sort things out. They will help frame the spot from which you can start to do the hard work of building a new triangle.

QUESTIONS FOR YOUR DEEPENING

1. What reactions are stirred in you when you think about the word "process" as it relates to your divorce recovery?

2. Which component of the marriage triangle faded for you first? Second?

3. Are you willing to build a new triangle to support your post-divorce life? If so, what obstacles might keep you from getting started or staying with it?

Chapter 4

Change Versus Transition

In my experience, what happens when you move from one thing to another is one of the universe's favorite tools. That's why it keeps coming up in your life. Right when you get settled into something, another shift starts to happen. And the spot between these shifts is a really active and sacred space if we allow ourselves some time in it.

With divorce, we can find ourselves in a spot where these shifts are happening back-to-back and sometimes simultaneously on top of each other. We would be well served by spending some time wrapping our heads and hearts around the ideas of change and transition. We may find it puts us in a better position to say yes to our new life situation.

Let's talk first about two words: change and transition. We use them somewhat interchangeably, but to our own detriment. Parsing out the difference between these two words can make a big difference in how you work through this difficult time.

In his book *Transitions: Making Sense of Life's Changes*, William Bridges describes change as something that happens *to* people. You get married, you have a baby, you switch jobs, you start a volunteer job, your husband loses his hearing, your wife loses her job, your physical abilities deteriorate. In your case, you get a divorce. These are changes. They are external. Changes happen *to* you.

Changes can be quick, and changes can be slow. But they all have a common impact in that our roles, our relationships, and our routines have been altered.

The change you are going through will require you to possibly visit with a mediator, hire a lawyer, talk with an accountant, consult a realtor, and sign countless forms. Divorce is a change that is changing your roles, your relationships (obviously), and your routines. There are many different books, seminars, and weekend events designed to help you manage the *change* that is divorce.

What William Bridges made clear, and you need to know as you walk through these days, is that every *change* is accompanied by an invitation to *transition*. Where change happens *to* you, in a sense externally, transition is *internal*. It's what goes on in your heart, mind, and soul as you are incorporating the change. If divorce is the change, transition is the transformation of your soul that can happen as you walk through it.

Transition is the inner-reorientation that happens. Transition is the self-redefinition that happens. And this inner-reorientation and self-redefinition are required to incorporate the change. The end goal of transition is acceptance.

Because transition is at its heart an invitation, it is also *entirely optional*. You don't have to do it. Notice I said that transition is the transformation of your soul that *can* happen as you walk through it. You don't automatically transition, and you don't automatically transform. You only get to those things by an intentional agreement to enter into the process and learn as much as possible from it.

Change Versus Transition

As an optional event, it should be said that we have all probably been close to people who experienced a change in their life and didn't accept the invitation to transition through the change. They passed on the invitation. And those people can come across as brittle, stiff, and even bitter about the change. Because the transition didn't take root, they are limited in their ability to move on. They got stuck.

You will get stuck along the way too. You don't hop from change to transition in a month. You move from change to transition to stuck to transition to stuck and on and on. The key is what you do with the stuck places. Stuck places can feel like the hopeless end.

At times, stuck places can encompass literal windows of time. The month of December. The summer. Last winter. But stuck places don't always operate in linear time. I find with both myself and my clients that the stuck places are more often topical. You get stuck revolving around an issue (or five). A sampling of stuck place topics: weekends without the kids, holidays, how it feels to drop off and pick up the kids, your ex's secrecy around how they spent their weekend with the kids, the new girlfriend, the fear that your kids won't want to be with you when dad is more fun, why can't he remember to send back the important stuff each weekend when they return to you.

You'll have these strong moments of really feeling like you can do this whole rearranged divorced life thing, that you've got your act together, and that this is possible. Then, a stuck place will trigger you into feeling as though it's never going to get better. You might spend more time than you wanted to on hysterics or shutting down in frustration, thinking "here we go again." The stuck places can really derail us.

63

For the heart that chooses to work at this, I want to assure you that your stuck places are not going to cement. They are always evolving. It's so easy to get fixated on relief that we fail to see the incremental progress we make along the way. The owner of a courageous divorcing heart needs to acknowledge the ways in which the transition is unfolding. You need to see that even though you are in a stuck place, it's not the same as the last time you were stuck. Your experiences have shaped you to be able to get unstuck once again, like you always have.

IT TOOK SEVEN YEARS

Since the divorce, my experience of the holiday season has been tricky. Dread and despair usually kicks off in October as I worry about which exact weekends people will host their caroling parties and whether I will have the kids. Or else, I fret about how in the world I will give my kids a shared Christmas morning that pulls us all together but doesn't leave me dying inside. With fewer days together to celebrate, how will I squeeze in all of our traditions and still have time to relax with them? I was stuck on these topics for 7 years. Seven years. Seven holiday cycles. I never felt like I was winning. Why could I not accept this new arrangement? Why was I still holding on to what it "should" be? Why did I lead with so much fear?

It didn't serve me to shame myself in these ways, and judging my own struggle didn't get me closer to my goal. What *did* help was my objective reflections on how each year did actually have a different tone to it. I just needed to keep track of the space between my transitions to recognize it.

Year One was the most beautiful disaster. Shockingly, my kids will still tell you it is one of their most favorite Christmases. It was my first divorced Christmas, and their dad and I had decided that I would enjoy the girls on Christmas Eve and until

64

noon on Christmas Day. My parents would be traveling up from Missouri to join us for my portion of the holiday. Then he would come get them, and I would crumble, and my parents would support me. That was my plan.

There were three gifts I was excited to give to my kids that year. First, I bought a big Radio Flyer riding horse for my youngest. Second, I purchased a larger-than-life stuffed bunny for my oldest. Lastly, I got a fish for the three of us to love. I know. A fish. But I was very allergic to dogs at the time.

The Radio Flyer horse did not show up at my door ready to ride, and I was horrified that it was shipped in what seemed like 4,532 pieces that required assembling. After my shock and tears, a co-worker offered up her son to put it together. I was relieved. The bunny was thankfully in one piece. And the fish, that was easy. Purchased, in a bowl. Hidden.

Well, the days leading up to Christmas Eve that year in Michigan were filled with lots of snow and lots of ice. There were power outages and threats of power outages. One outage happened three days before Christmas and the power company reported that power would not be restored at our house until after Christmas. Not cool.

In desperation, I booked a hotel and started to envision a divorced Christmas at a hotel. Was I in a Hallmark movie? I died inside. I put that gigantic horse and larger than life bunny in the back of my car covered in quilts and that sloshy water bowl with my fish in the front seat with my hand on top to steady it. I dropped a huge load of all of our presents and suitcases off at the hotel, exhausted. I panicked about Christmas at a hotel and went back to the house to wait with the girls until it got too cold to hang out there anymore.

And then, of course, the power came back on.

And so, I went back to the hotel and begged (as only a newfound single mom could) to be relieved of paying for that room. I loaded up all of the presents, and I came back to the house even more deeply exhausted. The next few days we continued with our traditions as a threesome. More snowstorms moved in. My parents announced it was too unsafe to drive up to be with us, and I realized we would be even more alone on Christmas than we initially planned.

Christmas Eve found us with a last-minute invitation to join wonderful family friends at a steakhouse before our church service. Driving home after the service, the snow kept coming down, and I cried. I cried for everything, because that's what you do in a divorce. But I was struck by how dark and beautiful the world was as I got closer to my home. It was really dark. Really a little too dark. It hit me as I got to the last block what was happening. The power was out. Again. On Christmas Eve.

I started crying harder.

And then, surprisingly, I was able to rally! Must. Save. Christmas. We will ENJOY THIS MOMENT IF IT TAKES EVERYTHING IN ME! I turned on my gas fireplace convinced it would warm us through the night. It didn't. I handed out the traditional matching Christmas pajamas for the kids and their American Girl dolls, and my oldest had grown since I bought them. They didn't fit. Now she was crying. We were all cold. It was getting desperate.

I called some family friends of ours. These friends hosted my Soup Group every other week, a gathering of families from my church to support each other and hang out. The husband of this couple lovingly and creatively remodeled my home with me.

I told him that I had no power, which I felt acutely in my heart. Also, I said, the power was out at my house.

He said he'd be right there. We loaded up the presents, that enormous horse, monster bunny, and a fish that was already feeling like he'd been picked by the least reliable owner in town. As we finished loading up these gifts now for the third time, I wondered aloud to my friend.

Why are you being so nice to me?

His eyes got big and his smile was wide.

Do you know the line from the movie Ice Age?

No, I replied.

He said, "That's what you do when you're in a herd."

I laughed and cried some more. I've never been more grateful to be in a herd.

What proceeded from there was what my kids remember: sleeping with his big family of four kids, confusion over what penmanship Santa really used, and the best Christmas morning breakfast either of our families had ever had. The power came back on, and the kids went with their dad to celebrate with him. I had everything that looked like Christmas put away by 1:30pm. I wanted a full day to cry and despair in a Christmas-free zone. I had dinner with some friends, and the next day was not Christmas anymore.

This was my starting place. It was not the glorious victory march that I wanted. It wasn't anywhere close, but I got through it.

The following year, it was time for the girls to spend Christmas Eve and Christmas morning with their dad. I started dreading that reality in March. As the day approached, I was graciously invited by the girls' dad and his girlfriend to come over on Christmas morning to be together as a group for the kids. Of course, I said yes and proceeded to dread it. Was there a theme here? Stuck much?

It was awkward. It was supposed to be, but I appreciated what we tried to do.

I brought the girls back with us to celebrate at our home, and the decorations were put away a day later.

What proceeded for the next 5 years were variations on that theme. Progress looked like pushing the start day of my dread a little closer to the actual holiday season each year. The decorations were put away a day later each year. Along the way, I put into place the four practices that follow in the next chapters. It was work. I was done up and done down more times than I can count. I stayed with it, and newness started to materialize.

This most recent year, although I brought dread along for the ride, I didn't start it until December, and the decorations stayed up past New Year's Day. The healing that I craved started to really take root in me this time. For the holidays this year, I'm aiming for a dread-free experience. I'm ready for it. I'm not stuck anymore. It was worth it.

It took me *seven years* to transition into this change. Seven. I don't say that to depress you, I say that to comfort you. I got one chance a year to practice transitioning into that change. I worked really hard. I got to the place that I dreamed of. It's possible. If I had let that first year be the guide for myself, I would have quit and stayed stuck. If I had let that second year be the guide, I would have quit and stayed stuck. But I didn't give up on wanting to be whole. My definition of whole is a woman who can experience change and then transition with heart right through the middle of it. The practices worked.

If you're careful with your process and your heart, you too will discover that all of the work you're doing will be worth it. As more and more transition takes root, even more growth can happen from the new space.

A warning: if you view the change in your life from the vantage point of "that person needs to change, apologize, or get their act together" or "this situation needs to be different or rearranged how I need it to be," then you are missing the invitation to transition.

My Year One Christmas story could have been told like this: "My parents let me down and didn't really try to get to me. My kids' dad should have showed up and helped us out. My friends should have dropped everything to make sure I was ok. I fell apart while everyone else had this perfect day. I needed the power to be on, the pajamas to fit, and the presents to be in one place until Christmas morning! Everything went wrong."

But the story I choose to tell is one that acknowledges that everyone was in a rough spot from that storm. The right people came into my family's dilemma at the right time on that day. And the memory of everything going wrong faded quickly into the comedy of the collective moments and the enduring power of friendship in that vulnerable time.

The story is different depending on where we shine the light. You hold the flashlight, my friend. The thing that needs to shift is in you. That is where transition really happens. Unfortunately, that is the thing we most often ignore or resist.

When we start shifting to some loving kindness inside of ourselves—instead of craving that our situations and the people in them would start to look differently—we can start to really crave that *we* could look differently *in* and with them.

The challenge then becomes a process wherein we walk ourselves back into the process of transition. By doing this, we take the time to investigate the invitation that a transition holds out to us and inject it with qualities that might make the shift desirable, purposeful, or headed somewhere deeper into the truth of ourselves.

It's overwhelming to take in. Let's break it down.

FIGURE OUT WHERE YOU ARE

First, you need to know where you are and where you are headed. Knowing where you are puts you in your reality. It breaks it down. I'm here. I see that I'm here. I acknowledge that I'm here. I want to be over there. I know I can't jump there. William Bridges' Transition Model for Change is shown in the curve below, and it is an easy way to help you find your heart and mind in a stuck place.

Endings	Transition or Neutral Zone	New Beginnings
Denial		Enthusiasm
		Trusting
Anxiety		Excitement
Shock		Relief/Anxiety
		Hopeful/Skeptical
Confusion		Impatience
Resignation		
Anger		Acceptance
Avoidance		Realization of Loss
Confusion		High Stress
	Conflict	
	Undirected Energy	
	Creativity	
RECONCILE	REORIENT	RECOMMIT

70

His three-stage curve starts with Endings, because all transitions start with the end of something. That ending is accompanied by a lot of emotions that we try very hard to avoid! Endings trigger anxiety, anger, and a tremendous amount of confusion. It's dark, and we have a lot of questions. Endings is where we see Sternberg's Triangular Theory of Love dismantling as Intimacy, Passion, and now Commitment fall away. As we move through the shock of endings, we move into the Neutral Zone. The Neutral Zone isn't defined by the panic of the Endings stage. Instead, it is marked by restlessness. It isn't as emotionally charged as the first stage, but it seeks to undo you with its in-between-ness. It's a sorting time, a "what works and what doesn't work" time, and you will want to rush it. Because what is our favorite part of transition? The end. Sadly, you can't skip the Neutral Zone.

Have you ever tried to lose weight? You do what you believe to be all the right things from drinking water to getting enough sleep to only eating when you are hungry. You get on the scale, hopeful after a week of sticking to your plan and realize disappointedly that you weigh the same as you did the week before. This might happen again the next week. Lots of people understandably quit trying after this feedback from the scale. Why bother working at it if nothing is going to change? If you stick with your plan, though, and you still drink the water and get enough sleep and only eat when you're hungry, maybe after that third week, you lose 2 or 3 pounds all at once. Why? Studies show us that when your body doesn't drop weight for a week or two, it's not being inactive. It's not rejecting your hard work, and you're not at a plateau. Your body is simply rearranging things on the inside. When things happen on the inside, we get super worried and sometimes lost wondering why our good efforts are not paying off more quickly on the outside. What we know about the body is that our health-supportive behaviors trigger a number of chemical interactions that prepare our bodies to drop more weight at one time instead of a little each week.

Picture the Neutral Zone in the same light as weight loss. You've gone through the Endings and it was hard. You suffered. You worked hard. Now you want to be at the finish line. This Neutral Zone feels like an inactive plateau of the heart that simply will not budge and let you get on with your life. What's really happening in the Neutral Zone, though, is a rearranging of things on the inside. And just like with weight loss, we feel worried and lost wondering why our good efforts are not paying off. What is actually happening on the inside, though, is that all of that intentional heart-building behavior is preparing to pay off in one large boost of relief.

We love the idea of being enlightened, and that's what we seek as we make our way into the Neutral Zone. But, as Barbara Brown Taylor reminds us, it is actually "endarkenment" that brings about true meaningful growth. We want to skip the dark, lost place. We want light and possibility and peace, while endarkenment and the Neutral Zone feel unmoored, without purpose.

You'll know you're coming out of the Neutral Zone when you notice you start to have some creativity. Not like scrapbooking and finishing that latch hook project. It's creativity around your situation. It's creativity that starts to ask whether something is standing on its tiptoes asking for attention so that you can move 1% closer to acceptance. The New Beginnings phase is willing to drop down into that deeper place of non-resistance.

When you start in Endings, as we all do, you typically dig in your heels. You don't want to go through it, and you resist any force that pushes you deeper into the curve itself. You flex your feet and push against the ground and feel like you're being dragged by a force outside of yourself. You want desperately to get back up on the top of that curve and never slide down! In the Neutral Zone, though, you bring it down a notch. You start to maybe kick your feet around. You stir up dust. You might even stand still for a bit. And toward the New Beginnings phase, you start to walk. One step at a time. You now know something better is available even if it can't be what you had before the Ending came to you. You suspect that there may be light (even if it's faint) at the end of your tunnel.

And as you walk slowly and carefully up that last part of the curve, acceptance meets you on your way. So does hope. And you'll probably squeal when you even get a taste of some enthusiasm. The New Beginnings zone is what you have worked so hard to get to.

In my case, with the holidays, I was ending what I felt was a classic, beautiful, perfect little family setting. I wanted all of us together like we used to be, and there really wasn't an alternative that was worth considering. I felt crazy amounts of guilt that I couldn't provide my kids with what I had grown up knowing. I carried tremendous anxiety about my own ability to handle the wild emotions of what the holidays would actually look like. I was afraid we would never be happy. I was angry that I couldn't have what I wanted. I was frustrated that I was such a mess. I was confused about how I ended up in this situation. My Endings phase was brutal, and I resisted every part of what that change was asking of me.

My Neutral Zone lasted many years. I kicked up a lot of dust waiting to feel better. I just knew my heart could get to a better place, but I couldn't get my heart to catch up to my mind's imagination. I tried all kinds of solutions. I let dread lead the way. I numbed out. I escaped, and I dove in. It felt like nothing was moving. I was destined to be robbed of any real abiding joy during the holiday season.

Then the New Beginning started to peek through. I started to notice that I had a line running through my head that kept me in the Neutral Zone. You've probably uttered it too somewhere along the curve.

My line was, "It shouldn't be this way."

This sentence was my banner. My identity. My song. To let go of it would be to not recognize my own life.

It shouldn't be that I am divorced. It shouldn't be that I am not with my kids during part of holiday break. It's shouldn't be that this is so hard.

It shouldn't be this way.

In mid-December during my *seventh* year of the struggle, I saw how that one line would keep me in the Neutral Zone for the rest of my life. If it shouldn't be *this* way, then how would I ever welcome the creativity needed to move up the curve to the new life I purported to crave? If it shouldn't be *this* way, what were we going to do with the fact that it was, in fact, this way?

I tried on how it felt to say the opposite. I tried saying, "It *should* be this way." I choked every time. No way! It *should be* that my kids suffer the pain of not having their parents equally available under the same roof? It *should be* that brokenness is acceptable? It *should be* that we all had to hurt so much?

As I did in my early days of confusion, I turned again to a spiritual friend. I told her all about how I couldn't wrap my head around letting go of this "it shouldn't be this way" line. I also told her how I knew instinctively that letting it go was probably the only way I would move forward. I couldn't get my mouth to honestly say the opposite.

"What if it *could* be this way?" she asked. "Maybe it *shouldn't* be this way. But *could* it be this way?"

I relaxed a little bit in that word "could." It *could* be this way. I *could* learn to make this work. I *could* try to find the places of lightness that were tucked in it. I *could* see how it *could* be a life that *could* be enjoyed.

And within moments, I was in New Beginnings. My creativity woke up after a multi-year productive nap. It wasn't what she said that woke me up. It was the noises from my thoughts that were ready to be released from their cage after a lot of heart work.

In *Waking Up to this Day: Seeing the Beauty Right Before Us,* one of my favorite authors, Paula D'Arcy, wrote eloquently, "It's a large commitment to play the hand life has dealt us, and it takes courage to make unbounded brush strokes with our lives—living into ordinary moments that turn us upside down. But one day you simply agree to the terms of life, the movement and change, all the impermanence, and the absolute stillness underneath." Once I let go of the resistance, let go of that line that kept me in the Neutral Zone, I started moving again.

It was like I did all the right things but could never lose the weight until one morning I dropped several pounds. It was all in there, patiently rearranging itself, waiting to be released. I'm convinced if I let go of that "it shouldn't be this way" thought even one year earlier, I would have missed some important part in the waiting. I was right on time. So are you.

I don't show you this curve so you can outsmart it—or worse, try to convince yourself that you are somewhere you are not. I want you to know where you are. I want you to put yourself on the map that leads to healing. You're not in a swirl that never stops. You're not on a road to nowhere. You're not a hopeless mess. You're not going to be here forever.

You are in motion. Even in the descent, you are moving forward.

Richard Rohr, a Franciscan friar, author, and founder of the Center for Contemplation and Action, writes often about descent and ascent. He says we go up and we go down in life, and when we are down, we think we are never going up again. When we are up, we think we will never go down again. Part of transitioning well, Rohr explains, is knowing that the ups and the downs are temporary. They come and they go. They will never be permanent.

In the meantime, we lean on the stories of hope from those ahead of us on the curve. I used to laugh at people who would tell me I would probably get married again (I did). I didn't believe anyone who told me that the pain would get lighter (it did). I didn't believe that my kids would still laugh and love both their mom and their dad (they do). And I for sure didn't believe anyone who told me my experience of the holidays would one day be sweet (they are).

Just like my babies learned to walk and my dog finally learned to poop outside, my heart learned that the grief could actually fade. As you let go of your right to resist the injustice, your transition will emerge too. Don't give up.

We've got the present moment calling out to us, the process of in-between marked out, and the desire to transition well through the change. What's next? Now it's time to do the work of the four practices. The four practices covered in the remainder of this book are what will solidify your new triangle. They create the structure that so many post-divorce families never fully realize. Let's get at it.

Change Versus Transition

QUESTIONS FOR YOUR DEEPENING

1. Where have you experienced a change in your life related to your divorce? What do you need to invite yourself to transition into that change?

2. Let's celebrate the small and big wins. What changes have you transitioned into successfully thus far?

3. Pinpoint where you are on the Transition Curve. What does seeing that location for yourself cause you to now understand?

Stay classy Brandy ...

Chapter 5

Practice 1: Rise Above

Stay classy. This was my motto for my divorce. It came to me in the early days as the earliest whisper of choosing the better path. Why classy? It spoke to me of rising above and of putting a high standard on the way I behaved. As you walk through your divorce, this commitment to a high standard is your everything. It is the foundation that you build on. Developing a trigger response pattern that seeks to rise above is critical to your healthy survival. Unfortunately, it's also the piece that has gotten lost in our contentious grenade-throwing divorce culture. Your ability to rise above is a gift you give your loved ones and yourself. To succeed at it, you'll need to approach it as the new lifestyle that it is. I know you're not going to stay classy 100% of the time. Neither did I. You're going to have your tirades, your expletive-filled rants. But I also know that if you create an intention, you will rise to it.

For me that meant jumping ahead in my mind a few years. You see, you have to have something really beautiful to look forward to in order to make it through this heart-stretching, tongue-biting, brain-pattern-rearranging process. It won't be effective to do this hard work if you do not see the end of it as a worthwhile destination.

79

BEGIN WITH THE END IN MIND

We need to start at the end. For those of you with children, I recommend you picture the end as the wedding of one of your children. I know your kids may not get married. I know marriage is not the ideal destination for everyone. Let's not use marriage as the penultimate life arrival point. Let's use it as an example of an event that really matters and an event where you will be in the presence of your former spouse and in the presence of your children a year or more out from where you are now (for those of you with married kids, picture grandbaby arrivals).

Now, there are many ways that day could take shape. I've been to a wedding where the parents of the bride and the parents of the groom were both divorced. Not divorced recently, but divorced long ago when the kids were much smaller. The day was tense. You felt the hurt still there. There wasn't an ease in the relationships between mom and dad. Don't get me wrong, they were trying. Trying hard. But the long-ago hurts snuck through the smiles they put on. You could feel that this was one of the hardest days of their lives. It wasn't just hard to watch their kids grow up and get married, but it was hard to be together as divorced parents of those kids with each other.

You've probably felt it before too at a wedding or birthday gathering, or maybe you've had friends tell you stories of their parents. They are civil. They are courteous. They are polite. They (barely) hold back the deep painful thoughts and give their former spouse the courtesy you would give a stranger. It's stilted. It's hollow. It's awkward.

That's one way to picture it. Is that what you want your child's wedding to feel like for you? Do you want to be a cauldron of difficult thoughts eking out supportive smiles and small talk with the person who helped you make this amazing child? Do

Practice 1: Rise Above

you want to resent that your child's other parent is there? Do you want to be huffing and puffing about your tired story of injustice as your child takes marital vows? Do you want to be stuffing down how much you resent the way your child's other parent made so many things difficult for you in this life?

You will ruin your day. You will likely ruin some part of your child's day too, as your unrest is detectable. You very well may cause those around you to feel uncomfortable as they watch you work overtime just to be pleasant. Is that what you want your child's wedding to feel like?

I hope that your dreams are bigger than just surviving and getting through that day. I hope your dreams are more beautiful than putting up with your former spouse and giving fake smiles when you're together. I hope your dreams aren't filled with dread as you lead up to the day or filled with tension that even other people can sniff out.

Let's dream better, shall we?

I'm not sure what prompted it, but early on in my divorce process, the idea of "rising above" got lodged in my head. In all honesty, it probably was motivated from the need to win rather than something more noble at the outset. I may be getting divorced, but you will never see me lose my cool again, I thought. I will rise, just watch me. Thinking like this made me feel like the victor. It was part vindictive, part pretty great idea.

I looked at my girls, and I thought about the future. I very much want them to be able to tell the story of their mom recovering from and living with the aftereffects of divorce with beauty. When I meet my kids' future boyfriends or girlfriends, I want them to be able to tell the story of their parents with me in the room. I didn't want anything shameful or embarrassing to be a part of that retelling. I wanted to be the heroine of that story. I

81

wanted their new partner to feel comfortable in our family as it was now shaped. But more than that, I wanted my daughters to be proud of me—so that they would never feel like they needed to hide my crazy in a secret conversation with their new partner. I didn't want my girls to have to warn these potentially new family members to avoid the divorce topic with me or avoid talking about dad around me, or worse, talk about their childhood with a great deal of pain around the family dynamics I provided them.

This idea of picturing myself at their weddings seemed like a smart way to see where I wanted to be, even though I was so far from it when I started out.

My imagination of the wedding started with Mr. H walking them down the aisle. I wanted my tears at watching that walk to include meeting eyes with their dad for a shared moment of delight that we were there, with her, and so at peace. I wanted to meet my daughter's eyes with overflowing joy. I wanted people to notice me for my joy and my fullness in that moment. I did not want to resent their dad. I did not want to throw a pity party for one. I did not want to withhold my heart. I wanted it to leap out of me.

I pictured Mr. H and I sitting next to each other in the pew. I pictured me wanting to make sure we sat together. I pictured myself at the reception, beaming as they shared a daddy-daughter dance. I pictured us dancing a proud parents dance, smiling at each other for what we made, what we lived through, and what we gave to each other and to them.

At my best, I wanted to know that I did everything I could to nurture my girls into a relationship with the best parts of their dad. I wanted assurance that I didn't limit their experience of him or their love for him. I wanted to know that I helped translate him at his worst.

Practice 1: Rise Above

My girlfriend Jen and I came up with a saying in our twenties: don't go to the hardware store to buy lipstick. It was our shorthand way to explain how we were starting to understand our friendships. If a friend is amazing at challenging you, but less than skilled at supporting you, don't call that friend up when you need support. Call the supporter friend. Go to the hardware store for the hammer. Go to the makeup counter for lipstick. Go to the challenger friend when you need to hear the truth. Go to the supporter friend when you need a soft place to land.

We get to teach our kids the same truths around their other parent, and if courageous, even ourselves. My kids know in their deepest hearts what they can count on from their dad. He can make them laugh like no one else. He loves to play with them, and he loves to relax with them. He can give perspective to their anxious and stressed hearts. He's a night owl and ready to take on the late hours. He can snuggle and make it all go away. He loves a good ski trip, and he is skilled at helping them see the other side of an argument. And he will be the first to tell you, he might not show up on time. He might have his head in a million different thoughts. He has a lot of work to do and can't always be where he wants to be. My girls go to him for the things he can give. Knowing these things helps me strengthen the Intimacy arm of my Divorce Triangle. It keeps me focusing on the parts of my former partner that serve our situation immensely.

The same is true for me. They can count on me for that priority listing in life. They know they are first, and I seek to be available. They know I will help them find the words to communicate tricky things. I will always be on time and usually sitting in a front row seat. And you know what else? I'm terrible at playing and chilling. My daughter asked me to put a chair in my bathroom for her because I'm always on the move and that's the only place I'll stay put for long enough for her to talk with

83

me. I can't sit and can't rest (I'm learning). I'm less touchy, more feely. I go to bed early and can't offer any goodness after 9pm. My girls go to me for the things I can give.

How did they learn this? They paid attention. But I also took seriously my role as Chief Glow Stick of our differently shaped family. Making sure that my kids had a dad even though I wouldn't have a husband was a value of mine. It was not easy. At first, I felt that he did not deserve it (that feeling has changed). But *they* did (and he does now too). My girls deserved to have an uncomplicated, unfettered relationship with generous access to their dad. They needed free access to everything that he is and everything that he isn't. This is because we learn relationships at home. They need to understand these "don't buy lipstick at the hardware store" concepts with us, so they can use them with their grandparents, cousins, co-workers, friends, and future spouses.

Back to my vision of the future: it was largely centered around my children and their wedding days. But, this works for any event: birthday parties, graduations, soccer games, and so on. Pick something that would be an internal emotional disaster if you attended it today. Set out the vision, and then get to work.

THE SWEET SPOT

The work that you can do to transition well in your divorce—the practices, the mindsets, the shifts, the postures—all flow out of one important relational concept: differentiation. Don't panic. It's a long word with a simple meaning. I learned about it during my divorce and was fortunate to spend a week in Colorado studying it from one part of the couple that popularized it, Dr. David Schnarch and Dr. Ruth Morehouse. Clinical psychologists and authors, Schnarch and Morehouse lay out differentiation as the careful balance between our longing to be independent and

Practice 1: Rise Above

our deep desire to connect. It's our combined love of being an individual and our love of being in good relationship with another. The balance between the two is the sweet spot from which we want to live. When we are differentiated, we are able to move toward and away from relationships in healthy ways. We have a self, and that self can stand alone comfortably. We have a self, and that self can move toward others comfortably to connect.

I like to call it living from your sweet spot. Everyone has their own sweet spot, and it looks different for each of us. As someone going through a divorce, it's important to know what yours looks and feels like. I know I am in my sweet spot when I'm grateful for all of the elements of my life, when I allow others to be as they will be, and when I offer myself fully in connection to those with whom I'm in the room.

Regardless of the shape of yours, what we all have in common about our sweet spots is that it is easy to tip one way or the other and get out of it. Just as much as you need to know what it looks like to be in it, you need to know what it looks like when you get tipped.

You'll know you've tipped when you are fearing you have lost your freedom or your sense of self and you feel trapped in a relationship. You might feel that you can't express yourself because you're tied to this former partner who keeps bringing you down. You start to complain that you'd be so much stronger, more relaxed, more successful and at peace if your former partner would just stop getting in your way and dragging you down. You keep trying to put yourself out there as independent and look for more ways to exert your freedom. You fear loss of autonomy. You fear loss of yourself because this trap of a crummy relationship is pinning you in. You get distant because getting close is useless and limiting and doesn't match with where you want to go. You pull away because your former partner doesn't get you and where they are doesn't fit you. You may have tried over and over to make it work, make it gel, and because of less than inspiring results, you withdraw. You just want to be you and not be hampered by them. You cry out for space. You can't look at the relationship anymore because it slams up against to the ways in which you see yourself in the world.

You'll know that you've tipped the opposite way when you start fearing your relationship to another person isn't committed enough or loving enough or secure enough. With your former spouse, this means you feel you aren't getting enough acknowledgement, attention, or response. You complain that you'd be so much stronger, more relaxed, more successful and at peace if your former partner would just meaningfully connect to you about the kids. You fear a loss of attachment and desperately need to get this co-parenting thing right. You can't be fully yourself because of this hollow relationship where you don't get your needs met. You see other people doing it right and wonder why it can't be like that for you. You want validation, something, anything to affirm that you and your kids matter to this person and that they are willing to work at making it better. You keep stepping in more and more and not getting the connection for which you long. You read books, articles, and talk to girlfriends about what a post-divorce family relationship could be like. Is it this? Is this enough?

It's *normal* to get tipped. When you are tipped, you either want more or less of the relationship. You can tip in either direction depending on what's going on. Tipping is often brought on by triggers: these little hot buttons that throw us off kilter. We sense micro and macro aggressions and react to them instinctively. While your sweet spot has some give and take to it, in divorce, you might actually swing wildly between being tipped one way or the other. The work is to manage the tipping, so that

86

Practice 1: Rise Above

you have a less destabilizing experience when it happens. We want to flow with the movement, and not get tossed about so uncontrollably.

Schnarch believes, and I concur, that the most important task in adult relationships is the development of a solid sense of yourself. This flies in the face of conventional wisdom, which teaches us that the most important things in relationships are communication, honesty, commitment, and empathy. What Schnarch teaches is that it is only within the context of your having developed a solid sense of self that you can encounter others in relationship well. Your solid sense of self is the basis from which communication, honesty, commitment, and empathy can emerge. Learning how to hold onto that self while engaging in a relationship, whether married or divorced, gives you a far greater chance of not getting tipped.

What's the big deal about getting tipped? When you are tipped, you are hyper-focused on getting your needs met *in reaction* to another person. For example, if you've tipped into feeling trapped in the relationship or suffocated in some way, your inner dialogue is scheming how to get some mental space from your former spouse. It's blaming them for being so insufferable and thinks if they would just get a therapist to sort out the issues then you could breathe again. It's reactive. You don't feel that way around your other friends, just your former spouse. You are reacting to a person and not creating a reality from inside yourself.

For those of you who tip toward freedom, your growth spot is realizing your former spouse doesn't give you the freedom you crave. You give it to yourself. This may have happened to you if you asked yourself things like this: "Will they just stop bugging me and stepping in with opinions all the time?" or "Why do I always need to do what they are suggesting, and it never works?"

87

Conversely, if you've tipped into feeling like the relationship isn't giving you enough stability, security, or affirmation, then your inner dialogue is working out ways to say even more clearly to your former partner, "I just need you to acknowledge me/appreciate me/notice me/parent with me." This type of thinking is blaming your co-parent for not filling up your emotional cup and not acknowledging you in the ways that matter to you. This is also reactive. You are not creating a reality; you are relying on another to give you the materials you need to make it. For those of you who tip toward connection, your growth spot is realizing that you can't demand that others connect to you. You want to be noticed, acknowledged, respected, and heard. You'll say things like, "If they would just lean in and listen to me and we could work this out for our kids" or "He's just not here. I try and connect, but he's so vacant."

Reactive living against your former partner will not generate the kind of free, whole, stable, or bright life that you want to live. It will halt your steps toward rising above. Almost all of my clients long to be less affected by their former partner. They don't like being rocked. They don't want to be yanked around emotionally and internally. They get frustrated that they keep having the same responses to the same situations and don't see themselves getting free or growing.

I tell them as I will tell you: it is possible. Becoming differentiated from your former partner, learning sweet spot living, is a lifeline for yourself and for your kids. But how do you do it?

My divorcing friends, if you're reading this book, you are wanting to figure out how to create a great family post-divorce. If you're going to be handed this unwanted life curve, you're definitely going to try to get somewhere beautiful. You try (and try and try) to build a relationship with your former partner. You try to document via text and email, you try to offer good

Practice 1: Rise Above

things to the situation, you keep going even when you want to quit. I want to truly acknowledge all that you are doing and doing well.

But here is where you will get stuck. I got stuck here, my clients get stuck here, and if you can get unstuck from here, you get to write your future. Your great relationship with your co-parent has nothing to do with the other person. Nothing. Nothing at all. And when you can incorporate sweet spot living, live fully from a differentiated and self-regulated place, you will be in the untipped, unhooked, untriggered life for which you have been longing.

You don't get to bring your former partner into it though. Yes, they are your material. Yes, they will present you with opportunities to learn (everyday). But they do not need to be willing partners in order for you to have a great relationship with them or for you to have a great divorce. Having a great divorce doesn't require the participation of the other person. Rising above doesn't require it either.

I know you think this is impossible and maybe not even advisable. But I've seen it bear truth in my own life and in the lives of my clients. The only person you need to work on is you.

As a young mom, I remember reading a book by Rudolf Dreikurs called *Children: The Challenge* that talked about how to manage the regular tantrums of a growing small child. The book came out in 1964, and some of the truths are still relevant. His bottom line was that you should take your sails out of their wind. What does that mean? It means that your boat doesn't move on the wind blown by others whether that person is a toddler or a former spouse. Your boat is commandeered and directed by you alone. When your former partner blows wind at you through accusations, inaccurate retellings of stories,

89

downright aggression, or silence, you are the one who turns your sails. *You* direct your boat.

You don't quit because they are doing that thing again. You don't get to say, "Well, I don't get the goodness because I have a rotten co-parent." You don't get an out. You have a very big in, if you want to take it. Your only job when you get rocked is to sit in, expand in, and grow in the very best version of yourself that there is. Hint: you haven't met this person yet. The person you will become when you can get your sails out of his wind is a person you will *love*. That person is the one who can do this.

PURSUING YOUR FOUR POINTS OF BALANCE

Schnarch lays out his four points of balance as indicators of an untipped life. These indicators are "life after divorce" goals that you can invite into your daily routine. Do so with regularity and I can guarantee you will get tipped far less often.

First is the development of a solid flexible self. You know who you are without others needing to tell you. You don't need social media likes, applause, or constant feedback to live your good life. You know your values, you live from them, and you don't need others to agree, change, or be better because of them. You're rooted. You can also adjust and change as you see fit.

The way you welcome a solid self is by conducting a thorough examination of your values. There are a whole host of values that might be important to you, but you can find your solid flexible self around four or five of them. Values like family, financial security, wisdom, freedom, pleasure, achievement, affection, authenticity, friendship, service, and responsibility drive our actions and impact what we want to present to the world. My values are family, personal growth, spirituality, and inner peace.

Practice 1: Rise Above

The flexible part of the solid, flexible self is the part that is growing, learning, and willing to own her mistakes and make course corrections along the way. She's able to bend and be shaped, while still adhering to the core values from which she lives.

Take a moment and identify the top ten values you treasure from this list compiled by the CDC Certified Divorce Coach® Program below:

- Family
- Happiness
- Health
- Competitiveness (winning, taking risks)
- Friendship (close relationship with others)
- Affection (love, caring, etc.)
- Wisdom (discovering and understanding knowledge)
- Cooperation (working well with others, teamwork)
- Fame (being well known or famous)
- Achievement (a sense of accomplishment)
- Wealth (getting rich, making money)
- Economic Security
- Financial Certainty
- Freedom (independence and autonomy)
- Integrity (honest, sincerity, standing for oneself)
- Inner harmony (being at peace)
- Creativity (being imaginative, innovative)
- Helpfulness (helping others, improving society)

- Personal Development (use of personal potential)
- Self-Respect (sense of personal identity, pride)
- Recognition (status, recognition from others)
- Advancement (promotions)
- Spirituality (strong spiritual beliefs)
- Loyalty
- Adventure (new challenges)
- Gender Orientation (strong identity to gender)
- Involvement (belonging, being involved with others)
- Economic Security
- Pleasure (fun, laughs, leisurely lifestyle)
- Power (control, authority, influence over others)
- Responsibility (being accountable for results)
- Order (stability, conformity, tranquility)
- Sexual Identity (having strong identity to sexuality)
- Culture (race or ethnic identity)
- Efficiency
- Effectiveness

After you've identified the top ten, see if you can whittle it down to five. With those five, write a statement about why you treasure each of the values. Detail why they are a motivation for you and why you uniquely are drawn to them. Bringing awareness to your values puts you in touch with what you want to organize your life around. If they are deeply held values, you will be compelled to bring them to life in all of the areas of your existence. Your values will come to bear on how you view your former

Practice 1: Rise Above

partner, how you create a new arrangement of family, and how you narrate to your kids this change in their world.

Second is the quality of a quiet mind and calm heart. When triggers abound, your solid self can quiet your mind and deepen into what you know. You can sit with chaos and not react impulsively. You know what you're made of, and you can bring your anxiety down to a lower frequency. These qualities are helped along by body awareness and knowing when our bodies have run away with the story our mind is telling us.

The way we welcome a quiet mind and calm heart is by working with our feelings. And the best way to work with our feelings is to ask kind, simple questions of ourselves. What am I feeling right now? What am I threatened by? What would it look like to have a quiet mind about this topic? What would it look like to have a calm heart in this situation? It's exiting the catastrophe train and taking a thoughtful walk with yourself. It's trading the thrill of the chaos and intensity of indignation and simply breathing. It's returning to the five questions in Chapter 2:

What am I scared of or anxious about?

How can I self soothe?

What do I need to confront in myself?

How do I contribute to my own unhappiness?

What is true today about me no matter what?

Take a moment and describe in writing what your quiet mind and calm heart look like at their best. That reality may feel so very far from you right now, but start where you are. If you can sense it, then you have a space you can start aspiring to. With a quiet mind and calm heart, you can respond intentionally to the myriad of tricky divorce situations in which you find

93

yourself. This is also how you strengthen the Passion component of your Divorce Triangle; you confront yourself and you learn to self-soothe in healthy ways. Often our quiet mind and calm heart emerge from both bottom up (bodily) and top down (mental game) work of regulation. Your body's wisdom to signal peace and the loss of it are important cues to honor.

The third indicator of a balanced life is grounded responding. Grounded responding takes the values you hold most important and communicates them to your audience with respect. You don't fly off the handle. You breathe through your reptilian brain moments. You see things for what they are, and you don't get your sails in other people's winds. You speak when necessary and are quiet appropriately. You don't explode, but you don't ignore.

As your best self, you welcome grounded responding as an overflow of your solid, flexible self and your quiet mind and calm heart. You cannot offer grounded responding from a self that is defined by the actions of others or a mind and heart that are untamed. You can offer grounded responding because you know your values, you live from them, you're willing to grow, and you're learning how to calm yourself down in triggering situations. Grounded responding offers your rooted response as an undeserved gift to whoever you deal with, including your former partner.

Take a moment and think through your most recent high-heated exchange with your former partner. With your five values, and your quiet mind and calm heart, what kind of grounded responding could you have offered? The fact that you can picture it means your heart can recognize the truth of it what it is to be this type of person.

Practice 1: Rise Above

The fourth and final point is meaningful endurance. This is your "why." Why you work, why you strive, why you keep going when it's easier to quit. It's the long-haul perspective that keeps you in the growth zone. Developing these first three attributes will not happen overnight. They will happen because it's Wednesday at 4 p.m. and you got an aggravating text, and you agree to step into the growth zone and unpack your feelings. You stop and think about your values, you calm yourself down, and then you respond from that new place. And you will do it, because you have your own unique reason for wanting to do it.

Try writing down your "why" to explain to yourself why you bother with working and striving—why you don't give up. It *is* a bother. It *is* hard work. Why are you in it? Why do you want more from yourself, your life, and your divorce? What drives you? You cannot make progress without your "why" firmly in place and revisited regularly.

Returning to these four points of balance gets your tipping heart back in the upright game, and it supports you in your efforts to rise above. When I imagine the weddings of my daughters and how I hope to participate in those big life moments, I can see that I have very "un-tipped" descriptions of myself. I am both free and connected. I'm both free to be myself and free to connect generously with my girls and their dad. I'm stable in myself, and as a stable self, I am able to connect in select places with their dad. Select places. I didn't envision us staying up all night telling each other our secrets and braiding each other's hair. I'm offering connection to him in select places—one in particular, our daughters. I'm connecting to the fact that his DNA, his strengths, his weaknesses, his flat feet, his gregariousness, his intelligence, and his love of the spiritual realm all passed on in varying intensities to our daughters. I'm

95

whole in myself and I want to offer myself to connect with him on this heartfelt shared topic in our lives.

The destination where I see myself arriving is untipped. It's self-regulating and rooted in responding in ways that are driven by the values that keep me going. I'm absolutely fanatical about getting to that place. I will, and do, take massive actions to ensure that I get there. I ask myself daily:

What do my values ask of me today?

What issues do I need to process to live from a quiet mind and calm heart?

What would grounded responding look like for me today?

WHAT TO DO WITH THE PAIN

But what throws me off the beautiful game I just laid out?

Pain.

So much pain.

So much mental and emotional stress.

So much suffering.

During the first part of your divorce experience, you rarely go a day without it. You hate it. You resist it. You wish it would go away.

It sucks.

In typical fashion, we believe that relief from our pain comes from what our soon-to-be-former partner should do or should stop or what we could do, say, or be to make them different.

In divorce, you have the opportunity to learn the true meaning of the phrase "Pain is inevitable, suffering is optional."

96

Practice 1: Rise Above

You will have pain. Your heart will break in a million pieces for yourself, for your kids, for your future, and for everything you ever understood of your past. Pain is not a bad thing, although it can feel like it. You will have suffering if you need everything to change but you. You will have suffering if you think you will never get to a point of freedom in your divorced relationship. You will have suffering if you keep using your former partner as an excuse for why it's so hard.

Let's let the pain flow. Pain, at its core, is simply an invitation. It's not a coveted invitation, but it is an invitation, nonetheless. Pain says, "Hey can we spend some time over here? Something is not right here, and I'm concerned." Pain raises its hand. It stands on tiptoe to get your attention. It notices when something is off. It raises a finger to suggest that there's more work here. The work is not necessarily to make the pain go away, but it is to let the pain occupy the space *without* the suffering.

Our poodle dog, Winston, is the official noticer of things that are off at our home. One night, I found him barking at our back door as though a team of burglars were ready to break in. As I let him out to go explore what he sensed, I watched him walk straight out to the pool. The wind had blown an inflatable flamingo pool toy into our pool, and Winston was not going to have it. He barked like management needed to attend to this deviation right away.

This is what pain does for us: it notices changes and it demands our attention. It picks up on subtle ways that things moved. It feels the ache of a weekend home that is empty, it frets about holiday plans with two addresses, and it hurts when a kiddo just wants her dad and he's not there. It's painful. Divorce is painful. But we can learn to allow the pain to be our guide, not our alarm.

As poet Maya Angelou said in her book of the same title, "Wouldn't Take Nothing for my Journey Now." This pain, the thing you most want to push away, has the potential to become the most important thing to you. It is for me. I wouldn't take anything for what I learned on my journey to this place. It hurt. It wounded. It took everything from me. And it gave that and more back to me. I wouldn't be the wife, friend, mother, daughter, and divorce coach that I am now without pain as my finest teacher.

So, let's be attentive students in pain school. Let's learn differentiation, sweet spot living, quieting ourselves. Let's rearrange the furniture of our mind to invite new things to sit there: possibilities, a strong solid flexible self, grounded responding, and ultimately hope. Your work at rising above will pay off immense dividends, and your investment needs to start now.

QUESTIONS FOR YOUR DEEPENING

1. Look back at the short list of values you created. Where are you out of alignment with them as it relates to your former partner? What would it look like to align your values with what you are trying to create for your post-divorce family?

2. What process do you currently use when you get triggered by your former partner or your divorce situation? Is it working for you? What new techniques could you try instead of or in addition to what you're doing now?

3. What is your why? Why are you pursuing something different and healthier than the normal course of events after a divorce?

Chapter 6

Practice 2: Own Your Part

You might not want to commit to doing another practice after living day-to-day with the raw and cutting pain of your divorce process. You are certainly welcome to not go any further. Many do not. To go further will require a likely unwelcome level of humility and grace that many of us simply don't want to access. To move through, and with, the pain toward this new practice, (notice I didn't say move past the pain) you will need to glimpse and be drawn to what it means to make peace with your former partner and with yourself. Peace is such a coveted word during this crazy time, and I know that it appeals to many of you. To get to peace, though, you will need to go on a longer journey and commit to a deeper knowing than just allowing the pain. Owning your own part is the start of that journey, your second practice in this long and instructive peacemaking process. It will fortify the Passion component of your Divorce Triangle as you pursue the self-growth that flows from facing this difficult task.

BUT IT'S NOT MY FAULT

Think for a moment about how hard it is for you to own your part in what you did to co-create the divorce situation you find

99

yourself in right now. Reflect on the level of difficulty you experience when it comes to truly apologizing for some part of the deterioration of your marriage. If this kind of apologizing is relatively easy for you and doesn't trigger a great deal of resistance in you, I offer my congratulations. The practice of owning your part may be something you can walk into with the hope of simply deepening in your understanding. For those of you who are more hesitant with your apologies or not able to see how your behavior contributed to the situation, then the path may be more of a struggle. I'll help you out.

Very few of us want to take the time to get past the things our former partner did or didn't do to us to get us here. Put simply, it's mostly their fault. In fact, a lot of the time we think it's *all* their fault. We say that, and we believe that in all honesty. We look objectively at the situation and conclude the same thing over and over. They never put down their phone long enough to talk! They were never appreciative! They rarely parented! Their anger was so difficult! It's not ok to be married and flirt with other people! They lied! They spent so much money!

You go out for a drink with friends and they too confirm it's all your former partner's fault. Friends love to pile on. That's why they are your friends! Now it's not just *us* assigning blame. If our friends see it too, then, hello—vindicated. Your friends will understandably process your divorce situation with the express desire to help you feel better. This is not a bad thing—you need them more than ever now. But at some point, you will also need a mirror, and friends are not going to be as useful in holding up the mirror for you. For your friends to hold up a mirror during this time is risky for them and for you. Any implication on their part that you are at fault in some way—and that your friends recognized this as it was happening—opens up all kinds of

Practice 2: Own Your Part

questions and misunderstandings. Why didn't they tell you earlier? Do they still want to be friends with you? How could they be so heartless? The shame and embarrassment are too much. The mirror needs to be in your own two hands.

It is definitely much easier and safer to stand in judgment of the other person than to look in the mirror or turn the courtroom toward ourselves. Most separating spouses don't even consider this particular practice. We enjoy our one-dimensional view on the topic. It is the only path modeled by most divorced people. Identify and blame... the other. If that's you, I offer you grace. It was me, too.

I felt it was all Mr. H's fault in the beginning. I was a victim like no other and I played it well. My list of his faults was endless. I went back and forth on whether or not to spell them out here. Doing so violates my own commitment to only speak publicly about my own contribution to our divorce. In light of that, let me give you Mr. H's part in his own words:

> In an effort to help readers put Andrea's story in context, I offer some reflections and learnings on my side. Chief among my flaws was a tendency to want to appear more enlightened than I was. That meant I would often hide my negative feelings from myself and others. Spiritual people don't get bogged down in negative emotions, I wrongly reasoned.
>
> I was a pleaser, a helper, and an approval seeker. I wanted to be liked. As a result, I would posture, mostly unconsciously, in a way that I imagined others would respect. Added to this, my job as a pastor further enabled a bit of a martyrdom complex. The story goes something like this: "Jesus suffered and forgave, I should do the same." It's good in theory; the only problem is I'm not

Jesus, nor one of his relatives. So, I didn't look honestly at my own limits and deal with them.

When I was unhappy with something in the relationship, I would bring it up, but if Andrea was reactive, angry, or unreceptive, I found myself softening my complaint immediately. Or, I might just slide under or around her in an effort to manage her emotions instead of deal with them or her directly. If she escalated, I became Jell-O. I did not have the courage to stand up to her intense emotions. I was a classic "nice guy."

But a "nice guy" isn't so nice in reality. My inability to muster a backbone was fundamentally unkind. It was unloving and a disservice to Andrea and our relationship. At the time, I even convinced myself that my complaints weren't that important. In doing so, I was deceiving myself and her in the process.

The reality was that our plane was losing speed and altitude fast. But I presented a dashboard that showed we were still doing ok. Yes, I signaled warning lights, but they were in the periphery, and I made them easy for her to ignore.

By the time I made my Proclamation of Disconnection, as she calls it, I realize it must have felt like a wrecking ball from out of nowhere to her. I remember her surprise and how sad it was we had co-created this moment. I didn't realize she didn't see what I saw. In that moment, I didn't understand my part in the story.

In the end, my lack of courage to be upfront pushed us to an edge from which we could not walk back. I failed to voice my legitimate grievances loud enough for a productive conversation to happen in time. I have

Practice 2: Own Your Part

owned this part of my story, apologized to Andrea, and learned to forgive myself so as not repeat it.

It was all his fault! Sure, there's more story, much more story to all of this. But, like you, I don't need much of the story to start on my "it's all his fault" tirade. When I slowly realized that his inactions and fears were threatening my sense of family, I threw fault in his direction like it was my job.

How dare you leave me on the outside for so long!

How does keeping secrets help a marriage?

Grow up and show up! Speak your truth! Value me enough to fight for this!

Why didn't you protect your heart and pull in others who could wake me up?

Why didn't you tell me right away what was going on so we could face it and make some course corrections?

I'll stop there. Because you know I could keep going. There's very little that stops a good tirade. We have some strong built-in equipment in us for blaming. I'm sure you can quickly find your own reference point back to your last blame session. We never plan for them, but my do they energize us!

And even though blaming comes so easily to us, we know deep down that it's ugly. It makes us look so very small. So then why do we keep doing it? Well, first of all, it helps us maintain our coveted victim status. And when we are the victim, we get pity. And some part of us wants that and likes that. Second, it feeds our story. Divorces are all about the story, and if you're human, you want the story to be that it's not your fault. Repetitive blaming keeps us safe from an unflattering story. Lastly, it's a great way to avoid owning your part. If you keep the attention on

103

your spouse's part, then you get a free pass from having to dive into what you might have done to bring about this situation.

When we first consider Practice #2 Owning Your Part, most of us bring a great deal of experience with doing the exact opposite. That's why I call it a practice, because owning your part is really going take some practice.

We typically approach the suggestion to own our part with a variety of reactions:

Some of us don't know where to start: *"This seems too hard to figure out and how important can it be anyway?"*

Others stop at a simple explanation that doesn't really get to the core of it: *"This is my contribution—I was hard to live with. That's it."*

We make our former spouse's lack of reaction an excuse for our part: *"Yes, I was probably hard on him. He just never told me that I was hard on him. How was I to know?"*

Sometimes we lean on the if/then to make our part seem unavoidable: *"Well I certainly wouldn't have stonewalled her if she wouldn't have treated me with such disrespect!"*

And for those of us who really have an aversion to introspection, we would just rather our spouse provide us with the list of our part: *"If she really is unhappy with me, then just tell me what I was or wasn't and what I did or didn't do to get us here. It's more efficient and accurate that way."*

There is also a legitimate resistance to looking at and owning your own part when you think your partner will not return the favor: *"If I admit to the part that I contributed, and my former partner doesn't acknowledge his part, then it looks like it's all my fault. Which is patently untrue."*

Practice 2: Own Your Part

Then there's the mother of all reactions. An affair. If an affair was involved, you feel you've got a free pass out of owning your part. What part could you possibly have to own? You didn't introduce them and offer them a cozy bed: *"His affair, his inability to be faithful, his cheating, his fault. Those are his actions, and they are not my fault."*

All of these responses are perfectly fine places to start. With the amount of hurt, overwhelm, and general chaos you are walking with right now, I can easily offer you a tremendous amount of grace if you are starting with a response similar to the ones listed above. Starting where you are is not shameful, it's real. Real is the only thing you have to work with in a situation like the one you find yourself in.

WHY OWNING YOUR PART MATTERS

With all of that grace in mind, I will now issue you a word of strong caution. While you are absolutely fine to *start* here, please know that to *end up* here is dangerous. Dangerous. Not "not recommended." Not "unadvisable." Dangerous. I mean that.

The danger lies in what you will lose later on. To walk through your divorce process and ultimately describe your part using a variation on one of the above explanations will limit the amount of connection you are able to develop with the four most important future relationships in your life.

Four Future Relationships

1. With your newly divorced self

2. With your former spouse

3. With any children you may share together

4. With any future love relationship you choose to enter

The Four Future Relationships are the absolute foundation of your future. Sure, there are more relationships that your future will probably contain, like those with extended family, lifelong girlfriends, work friends, or shared relationships with friends nurtured during your marriage. Those relationships are vitally important as well. But these four, these are the chief ones. If you fail in one of these four, the consequences you will suffer are enormous.

What do the failure and consequences look like in each of these? There are many scenarios. Here is just a sampling to consider.

1. With your newly divorced self

    Like it or not, this time in your life is an invitation. As I've said before and will repeat, it is not a coveted invitation, but it is an invitation, nonetheless. The relationship in which you anchored your life—past, present, and future—is dissolving. The dissolution is taking with it so many things that you hold dear. But the one thing it can never take is you.

    The days ahead will likely involve a lot more solo time with yourself. For some of you, that will be a relief from the physical presence of your former partner. For others, it may be excruciating to spend that first long weekend without your kids and your familiar role. I know I felt completely unmoored in that first year. I was lost and anxious and dreaded my solo weekends. When alone, I waffled between intense workouts and too much buffering. I spent time at the mall and ran needless errands just so I wouldn't have to be in my home alone. Others walk right into another relationship to fill the space. I did that too.

    We all know in our heads that running from ourselves covers up the parts we don't want to face knowing. That doesn't

Practice 2: Own Your Part

make it any easier to stop and face them. In fact, running may frankly feel like a bit of a necessity at times. Why do we keep running? Because we don't want to feel *all* of the things coming at us. It's hard enough to feel the undoing that is divorce, but when you add in the negative feelings that owning your part will stir up, it just sounds like torture. But if you can stop running for even a small amount of time, and do some of this important work, you will find that owning your part will help you settle down into your life as it looks now. You will face yourself, live with some discomfort as you walk through the process, take responsibility, and with any luck, can start to look ahead to the next phase of your life.

Without it, you can just keep running. We know these people. They just want to feel good. They just want to move on. And yet all of their attempts seem to not land in any deep new reality. They float. They flail. They don't root. The consequence they live with is an unexamined life, which exposes itself through a somewhat trapped life perspective, lacking the freedom and energy that comes from self-awareness.

2. With your former spouse

I've always thought the word divorce has this sort of final and distant feel to it. Like it's done, super done, super over, super out of your mind. Newsflash: it's not. Your divorce is part of your story. Your former partner is too. You do not "finish" your old life and "start" your new life like you finish and start a meal. I've always wrinkled my nose at the idea of a "new life." It's not actually a new life! It's a continuation of your existing life with different characters, addresses, titles, and table settings. For many of us, our divorced relationship will extend far past the number of years we were married.

107

As you know, the degree to which you interact with your former spouse is largely unique to your couple, work, and family situation. If you own businesses together and share children, your overlap is considerable. But even as a couple without those elements in common, you will likely not avoid your former spouse entirely. Sure, you may not live in the same city or run across each other in person, but the memories and the stories of your life together go with you.

For those with frequent overlap, especially those with children, your ability to own your own part takes a great deal of heat out of your interactions with yourself. Yes, yourself. If only to acknowledge that this rearranged and less than ideal life you now lead—with children getting dropped off, and bags of stuff being exchanged—is in part, made by you. If it is made by you, you can be mature, stop the blaming, and take responsibility to work on living it well. It redirects your energy toward the parts of your life that you can control.

Every action you can take that redirects energy away from your former spouse and back toward the space of your own life is an action worth taking. I cannot stress this enough. The more you target your former spouse as the source of all that is wrong with your life, you postpone moving on, and will likely add additional hurts to your relationship story. Without the conscious choice not to, you will carry your divorce forward and establish new routines of hurting each other.

Remember, while you have been busy nurturing the story that it is all their fault, they have had plenty of time to nurture their story that it is all your fault too. When you own your part, you take your partner's arguments and find places of agreement. You own whatever part of the truth that your

Practice 2: Own Your Part

partner experienced of you. You honor that they had an experience of you that you did not intend and that maybe you don't even agree with. You find the shred of truth that their story may hold, listen to that truth, and learn from it. And when you give your former spouse that acknowledgement—when you don't resist and deny their real story—you strip your partner of their power over you. They no longer need to spend their time convincing you of your wrongdoings. You own them. The temperature in the room goes way down. Your ability to function as co-executors of what overlap you still have in life goes up.

3. With any children you may share together

Out of fear of losing your children, you choose to believe that your spouse is largely responsible for the divorce. Their actions and inactions make this a clear-cut story and thankfully you are not at fault. You share this perspective freely with your children, subtly turning them against the other parent and ensuring you get as much parenting time as possible. You tell everyone you are sad that your kids have such a terrible other parent, while secretly loving it because it keeps your children close, keeps your holiday routines intact, and engenders pity from others who watch you single parent. Meanwhile your children grow up without the investment of the other person who made them or made them their own. Parental alienation is real, and it harms your children.

As your children get older, though, they will want to piece their own lives together and might reach out to the other parent. They may get information you might not have been willing to own about your part, and it rocks their boat and yours until everyone works (or doesn't work) it out. Your kids live in fear that they will repeat what happened to you;

The Best Worst Time of Your Life

they fear marriage and fear close relationships. You don't give them the narrative that you made your own mistakes, you owned them, and you are making a life that matters with what moves forward. You don't give them the upfront and personal gift of showing them that love is worth having and worth fighting for, and when love ends it can take new shapes.

Your children are learning from you how to react to hard things. If you want them to learn that other people make your life hard and you are powerless to change that, then go right ahead and trash your former spouse in front of them. If you want them to see in you a survivor, a person who can face hard things with grace and dignity, you may want to own your part and start shaping a story you want them to witness.

4. With any future love relationship you choose to enter

Let's say you continue to avoid owning your part in your divorce. You fail to dive as fully into the part you played in getting to the point where your marriage could no longer continue. You hold onto what you believe to be the truth: that your spouse caused this and you are the victim. Fast forward a year and you're dating someone. You enjoy a bliss you have never known, telling everyone how much happier you are now that you don't have to deal with your former spouse's issues. They are the perfect opposite of your former spouse and you're thrilled. You get married, and five years in, you're doing that thing that you didn't know you were doing. You still don't know you're doing it. Your new partner suffers in different but similar ways to your first partner. Slowly over time your behavior undermines the closeness you once shared.

110

Practice 2: Own Your Part

Alternately, let's say that you own your own part early on. You study yourself; you grieve what you were not or could not be for your former spouse. You offer compassion to yourself and your former partner, reminding yourself that everyone is in "life school" and you need to repeat some classes just like we all do. You experiment with new ways of living, try on some new ways of coping and relating, and step in with both eyes open to a new relationship. Your first date with the new person doesn't consist of you bagging on your former spouse, but rather on what you learned in the coming undone. You humbly offer yourself as a person who is trying to get it more right this time.

Hopefully this has inspired you to at least consider spending a little bit of time attempting to own your own part. If you're not convinced, I get it. You've got a lot going on, and right now that process may take more from you than you have to give. If you are convinced, though, let's get started with our practice.

Mr. H's and my counselor said at one point that no divorce is ever 100% only one person's fault. In the same breath he also said, "but rarely is it 50/50." Oh, how I wanted to bank on this possibility. Initially, I was willing to take a 5% fault to his 95%, easy deal. But what kept me from owning my own part was feeling like if I took more responsibility for my contribution, then it would give him leverage to leave. If I just hurried up and fixed all of the things that were on his initial list of difficulties with me, then the proof would be my new behavior. I would really do anything to avoid having to look at the past. Besides, what good is looking at the past? I'm fixing my future! I'm doing the better thing.

111

HOW TO OWN YOUR PART

Thankfully, my resistance was broken down. At some point in the counseling experience, I was able to face the prospect of owning my own part with regard to our past. It came pretty naturally after reading a blog post that summarized Dr. John Gottman's Four Horsemen of the Marriage Apocalypse. Dr. Gottman's thoughts on marriage had registered highly for me since college, when my Sociology professor told me he was the only one to trust on the topic. She said everyone else at that time wrote books anecdotally about their observations, where Dr. Gottman did actual brain research on couples. The Four Horsemen--Criticism, Defensiveness, Contempt and Stone-walling—are ways that all couples relate at times. Those who find themselves near separation and divorce have a much higher incidence of these behaviors in their relationships. I knew immediately that all of these behaviors got me into this mess.

I met my own resistance in taking a deeper look. I worried. What if it really was entirely my fault? What if I couldn't be a victim anymore? I didn't want to lose face. But even with that pushback I knew I needed to start in, start listing my own contributions and owning them in a new way. I needed to trust the process to change me. Somehow in my ignorance I lost the most important thing to me, my intact family. This is my story of how I lost it.

I started with Contempt. Contempt is the absence of admiration. Our marriage started out with my great admiration for Mr. H's way in a crowd, his leadership, his intellect, his intuition. I took for granted that he knew all these things. Surely, he knew he was great; I'll be the voice of critique instead. It wasn't conscious, but it happened. The things that needed to change in him or could use some tweaking were always first on the agenda. The things that were admired, well, he could handle those on his own.

Criticism:

Again, I paid attention to his shortcomings. I was very aware of what he wasn't. He was too much of this, too little of the other, too loud here, too quiet here, he wanted too much, he desired too little. I rarely let things slide. I pointed them all out. Grace and forgiveness didn't feature large.

Defensiveness:

I resisted any attack. I always had an answer for why it wasn't me that caused a problem. It was hard for me to say, "You're right; I am sorry." Anger and resistance were easier and felt justified.

Stonewalling:

At times I chose withdrawing instead of engaging. He wanted to talk about how I was failing him, but I didn't want to hear it. I didn't know *how* to hear it. And that was because I didn't know how I was going to change anyway.

A surprising thing happened to me in this process of reflecting on my part. I got really sad about my marriage. Sure, I had some behaviors that didn't support Mr. H. He owns that he had some that didn't support me either. But the marriage itself—that's the thing we both broke. This mystical union under our watch and care... it broke.

Reviewing these Four Horsemen is a basic, rudimentary, bottom-level, easy-access way for you to start owning your own part. List the horsemen out, and spend some time agreeing with how your behavior lined up with them. Be honest with yourself. It does you no service to sugar coat this evaluation.

I have a friend who really could not grasp, and maybe didn't entirely want to grasp, this concept of owning his part. He was pretty comfortable with how he acted and was convinced that his was a case of mismatch. He thought his wife had changed, and he had not, so there was not much to own. Because he liked how his life looked, how he was perceived and received by others, he had little to no motivation to enter this process.

Rather than start with the horsemen approach, I encouraged him to back into it a different way. I suggested that he picture himself entering a new relationship with a new woman. Then I directed him to spend some time thinking about all of the ways he conducted himself in his most recent marriage. Next, I asked him to make a list of all of the ways he behaved that he would like to again recreate in this new relationship. The next far harder part was to make a list of all of the ways he behaved that he would not like to carry forward into a new relationship. Some of those regrets are fertile ground for owning your part. It also directs your attention to a new relationship and keeps you from getting tangled and defensive in the old one.

Just remember, whichever tactic you try, you will likely encounter resistance from yourself while doing this. Congratulations! You're human. Keep going.

Let's revisit those Four Future Relationships for just a moment. Once you have uncovered the painful truth about how you co-created the situation you now find yourself in, you have the raw material to come from a very healthy, stable, and honest position from which to build the Four Future Relationships with yourself, your former spouse, your shared children, and your future partner. The key in each of these, is to only talk about your part. Whether you find that simple or difficult, it's vital.

Our counselor had many pieces of wisdom to share with us, and one that looms large for me relates to this directive to only talk about your part. He said if you only share your regrets about what you did to get yourself into this situation, you will avoid so

114

Practice 2: Own Your Part

much of what makes those post-divorce relationships suffer over the long term. You tell yourself you messed up, that mess up led to some big consequences, and you're going to make some changes and learn as much as possible through the process. You tell your former spouse that you can see how you made the marriage less than what either of you had dreamed it would be. You tell your kids that you regret what you couldn't be or couldn't do to keep your family intact even if it was based in pure ignorance. You tell your future partner that you're learning to grow and better yourself in all the ways that your previous marriage taught you. This is a mature story you want to be the center of! This is the kind of person our world needs! Lay down the weapons, stop defending your story, and walk with the confidence of a life examined into your next days.

The person who can do this is a person who, ultimately, can be humbled. But more so, it is a person who can give her/himself grace. Grace is funny, because it seems to be one of those gifts that we can only give when we receive it for ourselves. The measure to which you can give yourself grace is the measure to which you can offer it to others. Find ways to agree with your spouse about what you couldn't be. Find ways to carefully consider that what your partner says about you might be true. When you can look at your failings, honestly and humbly, and offer a heartfelt apology for how that caused a once loved person in your life to lose heart with you, you are at a very new place in the peacemaking process.

115

The Best Worst Time of Your Life

QUESTIONS FOR YOUR DEEPENING

1. Owning your part affects your four future relationships. Which relationship concerns you the most? What do you need to own from your own divorce story in order to prioritize that relationship going forward?

2. As you reflect on your marriage, when were you the person who chose contempt, criticism, defensiveness, or stonewalling as a way to relate?

3. Think on how you gave yourself to your marriage. Which parts of yourself do you want to continue into a future relationship? Which parts do you hope to abandon?

Chapter 7

Practice 3: Fight For Gratitude

Gratitude is a catch phrase. It's popular. It's easy to find it on T-shirts, wine glasses, and bumper stickers. Small problem, though: it's not that easy to find it in the midst of a divorce. Sure, you may be saying "I'm so grateful I'm about to be done with this mess," but true, deep, overflowing gratitude is not usually on the tip of your tongue.

Prior to my divorce experience, I had a casual relationship with gratitude. Of course, I was grateful for so many things—family, money, nature, good friendships—but it didn't feature large in my heart. Gratitude as a personal practice didn't emerge until the first day I met my spiritual director.

There's something weird about being married to a pastor. I do the laundry for this person that people respect, look to for guidance, trust with their stories and secrets, and listen to for what God might be trying to teach them. They put him on a pedestal; I put him on assembling the crib. They hang on his every word; I tell him to be quiet or he'll wake the baby. I learned a great deal from him spiritually, but I didn't get it from his sermons. I learned it from our life together. I saw behind the veil of the revered pastor's role and knew he was just the guy who hates mowing the lawn and really loves Spinal Tap. He was also

117

the guy who really wanted people to grow in their sense of the divine. This way of managing the dual roles made me feel that I had my pastor's wife head on straight. He's a spiritual gift to many, including me, but he's also and more so, just a regular guy to me. I made it work.

But shortly after the Proclamation of Disconnection, I realized my boundaries between the two roles, pastor and husband, weren't as distinct as I thought. My thoughts were all over the place:

"If a pastor is considering leaving me, then what does that say about me?"

"If the person who is supposed to love all God's people can't love me in our marriage anymore, then I must be really, really bad."

"If God can't give him what he needs to love me, am I unlovable?"

And the worst thought of all: "Maybe it's God who really doesn't love me?"

That one cut me. That one got me all worked up. Because what if God really did think I was unlovable? That's bottom-dropping-out stuff for me. I didn't see a way forward if that was the new truth of my life.

I knew it wasn't solid thinking, but I also wanted someone professional to agree with me. Several friends of mine had been studying spiritual direction at that time, and I thought maybe I should give it a try. If you're not familiar with this field, spiritual directors are trained to help you notice the movements of God in your life. They are skilled in contemplation and deep listening, awareness, discernment, the connection between your body and your spirit, ancient spiritual practices, and self-examination.

They are spiritual therapists for the soul and seek to hear with you what God might be nudging in your heart. It felt like a good starting place.

DEEP PEACE AND FREEDOM FOR WHO?

I began seeing a spiritual director, Judy, referred to me by a friend. Judy met me at the Dominican Center, a sanctuary of quiet in the city and where many go for guidance and training. She had white hair and a big smile, and she didn't seem as amped as I did when I walked in the candlelit room. I felt better just being in her presence. She laughed lovingly at my fear that God was leaving me, giggling at the thought that the divine could find me distasteful after all these years. She assured me I was in the right place, and that God doesn't quit on people. Her gentle wisdom was immediately believable, and I started to trust her with my story.

After she listened to my explanation of how I was stuck with this humiliating and unwanted likely divorce, she said only one poignant phrase:

"What if you wanted deep peace and freedom for Mr. H regardless of what it means for you?"

Ummmm, come again?

That question rocked me.

I didn't want deep peace and freedom for him; if I was honest, I wanted pain for him. At that time, I wanted him to suffer from as much or more pain as I had. I wanted him to lead a life full of regret and difficulty as punishment for what I was going through. Her suggestion was ridiculous, but it was also strangely appealing.

She said that love at its most basic essence is wanting deep peace and freedom for those around us. Love shapeshifts as it moves into different territories. It expands to address racial inequities, it nurtures the elderly in their last days, it helps parents launch kids into adulthood, and in all situations, it seeks deep peace and freedom on behalf of others.

You can't really argue with that. But embarrassingly, what I knew for sure was if that's the definition of love, then I am wildly head over heels in love *with myself*. My goodness, all I wanted was the deep peace and freedom train to stop at my house and take me on a forever ride. I'll pay the ticket, just let me on board! For Mr. H though? Really? That's deep. That's next level. I was hesitant but intrigued.

When I probed as to how I travel to this place of desiring deep peace and freedom for him, she offered a simple suggestion. She encouraged me to come up with three gratitudes for Mr. H every day. They were to be done before I got out of bed. They were to be original and there were to be no repeats. If I could commit to this practice daily, it might create an opening for a new way of thinking about him. Okaaaaaaaay. With trepidation, I signed up.

It was a daunting task. That first day—actually those first few weeks—were brutal. The most ridiculous, tiny, pathetic gratitudes reluctantly made their way out of me. Day One: I'm grateful he doesn't hit me, I'm grateful he doesn't do drugs, and mostly I'm grateful he's not here right now. Day Two: something about being grateful that he knows how to remove splinters, that he isn't disabled, and that he uses deodorant. My gratitudes were pitiful. They were largely centered around what he was not.

As I ran out of these low-hanging fruit of gratitudes, I noticed I laid in bed longer. My brain wanted to do repeats. I couldn't

Practice 3: Fight For Gratitude

find the gratitudes. My disappointment, my profound pain and hurt, and my anger would not let me be grateful for this man. These strong emotions resisted my best efforts toward gratitude.

The truth about divorce is that negativity is the natural course of events. We dismantle the intimacy, passion, and commitment that held us together. If you get up every day during the course of your divorce process and do nothing to intentionally reverse the normal flow, your heart will beat in an overwhelmingly negative cadence as you stare at what came undone. It will insist on revenge, justice, punishment, and fear. It will blame, attack, diminish, and quit. It might even just go quiet on you. It may go in the direction of defeat or quiet simmering. You'll find yourself saying "I'm so over it," all the while suspecting that this isn't what "over it" should look like. Let's be clear: it takes *enormous* intention and sacrifice to end up with a heart that sings anything but a "screw you" anthem steeped in an ever-growing desire for the other person to suffer greatly. It takes *time* to shift this mindset.

This practice of gratitude is how we put in place the new revised Intimacy leg of our Divorce Triangle. My own gratitudes, which started so feebly and only grew stronger, became the only thing that saved my heart. My fight for gratitudes took the other fight out of me. It felt very disempowering at first. There's a sick power that comes from being righteously offended, indignant, and sure of your right standing in a situation. This fight made me feel alive and made me feel justified. It made me feel strong to point out all the ways this guy failed me. In the end, though, that approach also really, really, made me feel like a victim.

You see, if the problem is always him—what he does to me, what he doesn't do for the kids, what he says, what he forgets— then my whole life was going to be lived in a reactionary state. If his actions and inactions are my starting place, then he's in the driver's seat of my life. I'm a victim to what he does and doesn't do. When I'm a victim, I can't be a creator.

Victims live in reaction; creators live in creation.

Do you see how those words, reaction and creation, are the same letters just switched around? You can spend your life reacting, or you can spend your life creating. It's up to you. But you don't get to create with hate. Hate blocks creation. Hate keeps you at a distance from your former partner, but more threateningly, it keeps you at a distance from *you*.

What I noticed when I pushed through my resistance to more meaningful gratitudes about him, it got weirdly soft in my heart. When I dropped into this new place that Judy had a hunch I might find, I was grateful for a lot of truly remarkable things. It didn't necessarily get easier, but it got honest. I took an outsider's perspective and tried to appreciate what others loved about him. I saw him as a co-worker and pastor. I took our kids' perspective and saw him in their light. I positioned myself as his mom and dad, reflecting on the gifts he brings to them. Those reflections made me so very sad. I started seeing things in Mr. H that I wish I would have celebrated more heartily when we were together. Gratitude softened my heart toward my reality and helped me acknowledge the assets of my partner alongside what wasn't enough.

It made me super angry. It really did. I didn't want him to be even a little bit awesome. It served my story more if he was a terrible jerk. In our earlier years, Mr. H would say to me that I loved the black and white stark nature of issues (he was right), but most of life and most people are in the grey. They aren't all bad. They aren't all good. They are both. I really wanted him to be all bad. That's the normal way of divorce. By doing this practice, my heart started giving equal airtime to the difficulties and the gifts.

Practice 3: Fight For Gratitude

For those of you starting on this most painful journey of an unwanted divorce, what does it feel like for you to consider wanting deep peace and freedom for your former partner regardless of what it means for you? I can already hear you telling me how I don't know your former partner. How your spouse is so very, very terrible. How your story is special and there's no way you could try it. Your circumstances qualify you for a special pass. Your spouse is a narcissist. Your spouse stonewalls you regularly. Your spouse left you for a younger version. I get it. I talk to a lot of people getting a divorce and what's true is we all think we have it the worst. It's true. You do have it the worst. You have it the worst for you. And that's your story.

YOUR PRECIOUS STORY

I'm not here to take away your story. It's yours, and you are welcome to keep it.

But something in you wants healing. You picked up this book because you wondered if now is the time for really getting to the bottom of this pain. If you're open to it, let's take a baby step away from your story. Let's make a small, measured shift of mindset that could support your deepest heart longing to just feel better.

When budding authors enter any kind of writing program, they are quickly taught to collect material. They're told to collect it from the outside world, from the inside world, from places, people, actions, inactions, thoughts, feelings, and observations. The process of sifting, sorting, combining, testing, refining, and developing this collected material leads ultimately to a story. A writer will also tell you that there is no story without material.

The Best Worst Time of Your Life

As a divorcing person, you are likely telling (and retelling) your story to any sympathetic heart that will hear it. Your co-workers, friends, parents, and the person in the seat next to you at the bar all get to hear you tell it. You've told it so many times that it's rehearsed. You bore yourself with telling it after a while, especially the part where you still feel bad at the end.

As any new author learns, though, your story at its core is really just your material rearranged in a way that gives it life. For a moment, step back and take a glance at the material with which you have made the story you're currently telling. If you're like many, no all, of my clients, the most substantive material in your story is your former partner. The material is your former partner, and the story you make is yours.

I have not met your former partner, but I can still tell you without knowing this person that they will never stop doing that thing that makes this so hard for you. They won't. I guarantee you they will never stop pushing your buttons in that exact way that you tell in your story. I also guarantee that they will keep reliably and predictably being the material for your story.

You could fill notebooks with the negative material your former partner has contributed to the story. You've got so many valid disappointments, parental failure, boundary violations, verbal insults, negligent incidents, and tales of disgust. You can write a very, very good story with this material. My friend, you have written it. So far it hasn't gotten you anywhere that you want to be. All of this material makes for a very sympathetic story to tell others, but it doesn't lift you out of your pain and overwhelm. It doesn't open you to new places of calm and relief. Most of all, it doesn't free you to walk with the lightness you crave in your future.

Your story is yours, but it's lopsided. It isn't the whole story.

Practice 3: Fight For Gratitude

It's a tremendous ask, and I wouldn't fault you if you said you weren't ready for this gratitude practice (and that your former partner didn't deserve it). But to start getting yourself to the place of freedom where your divorce and their demise aren't the only thing you think and talk about, to start getting to the place where you let this divorce make you instead of break you, you must be willing to enter into practices that make space for a softer, more willing you to emerge. That softer person is blocked by your story about your spouse.

You need to be willing to collect new material.

Under no circumstances will your soon to be or former partner ever "deserve" the kindness you generate through this practice. Don't wait for your heart to think that crazy thought. They deserve unending torture and shame, I know. But hear me out: it's way more about what *you* deserve. You deserve to not walk around with a load of hatred, rage, and disregard for this person with whom you will very much live out the rest of your days with, divorced or not. You deserve the very deep peace and freedom you're trying to generate for them.

Where does your deep peace and freedom start? It starts with the first practice of living into the process of differentiation and continues to expand as you employ the second practice of owning your part. It also grows bigger through gratitudes for this person. That allows you to get a clearer handle on the fuller person that your former spouse is, the "grey" of that person. With my clients, I help them explore all sides of the blessing and the curse of that person. Because you know what? That's your person. I know you're getting a divorce and you're going to move on in life and have separate addresses, but he or she is still going to be your person. Especially when you have kids. This person's wellbeing and downfall affect you tremendously.

125

Becoming an expert in all things "your person" is really at the core of what I teach my clients about how to inhabit a beautiful life post-divorce. It comprises the core of the Commitment component of your Divorce Triangle. In order to engage the post-divorce relationship in a way that builds your triangle, you need to learn all the ins and outs of your former partner's operating system. When you can really see the blessings and curses of your person—the gifts right next to the challenges—you are finally working with reality. Your reality. And making friends with your reality, aligning with your reality, and allowing your reality to sit untampered with in your heart is vital to your peace of mind. If you can only see the ways your person fails (to show up, to pay, to be kind, to parent) you will never give them deep peace and freedom, but sadly, you will rob yourself of it as well.

LIMITS AND BLESSINGS INVENTORY

So how do we get your thinking about your former partner into a comfortable reality, a reality that you can work with and not resist? It starts with an inventory of the limits and blessings of your person.

Take my client, Michelle, for instance. Her most common complaint about her former spouse was, "He gets in a big fuss about making this custody schedule with me and then last minute he either doesn't show up on time or says he can't make it at all." Then that's usually followed up by, "It happens so often, I don't know why his inability to honor this schedule surprises me." For Michelle, this way of thinking and talking to herself meant that every week, or every other week, she lost an hour of her life to extreme disappointment and frustration and emotional stress to this issue. She would stew days later about how he doesn't care about the kids and doesn't care about her and maybe she should take him to court (and added that she couldn't go out

Practice 3: Fight For Gratitude

with her friends like she had planned). She would call up a friend and tell her the story again and wonder how a guy who says he loves his kids can keep failing at the one thing he's supposed to do, which is to spend time with them. She was ready for a change.

Michelle also said a phrase I hear quite often among divorced women about their co-parents: "I just can't trust him." The simplest definition of trust is being able to believe in the reliability of a person. So, in Michelle's mind, if she can't trust her person's reliability to honor the schedule, then she can't trust him at all. We limit our understanding of trust when we think about it only in a positive sense. Reliability is at its root performing consistently. Therefore, isn't it just as true that Michelle can trust him to *not* honor the schedule? If trust is being able to believe in the reliability of a person, then doesn't that translate into her being able to trust that he will *regularly* dishonor the schedule?

My own counselor posed a different definition of trust that changed my perspective immensely. His definition of trust is that trust equals consistency over time. Trust is knowing what will happen because it has consistently happened over time. Thus, Michelle can trust her person. She can trust that he will not honor the schedule.

Why does this matter? It gets you one step closer to inhabiting your full reality. I'll add another formula to this conversation as well. I believe it is the simplest and most important formula for living your life post-divorce:

Limits + Blessings = Your Reality With Your Person

The Limits + Blessings = Reality inventory is a situational and ongoing effort. You won't start and finish it today. You might for one situation, but it is designed to support you for the lifetime you have ahead with your person.

127

It starts with the limits. Take note: limits are not feelings. Limits in this exercise are facts, facts regarding challenging things. I know you'll love this part. You've trained well for this moment! Michelle made this list of her person's limits in this child sharing custody situation:

Limits About My Former Spouse In This Situation

- He regularly can't keep his time commitment with the kids.

- He regularly is last minute with schedule changes.

- His schedule is unreliable.

- He doesn't say sorry when the schedule changes affect me negatively.

She can trust all of these things to be true because trust equals consistency over time. Over time, her person consistently behaves in these ways. The way you write the limits matters. Notice she didn't write that he can't keep his time commitment *because he does not care about these kids*. It wasn't that he is last minute with schedule changes *and I want to scream at him because it's a total inconvenience to me and rude of him*. It's not that he doesn't say sorry *and I'm so sick of his lack of regret*. It's factual. Make a list of factual limits.

Now it's time to turn the tables and examine yourself. What are your limits in this situation? What are you not able to offer? Ouch. This is the part you may want to skip, but trust me it's an important step on the way home to the calmer headspace you crave. For Michelle, that meant being pretty honest about what less than lovely things the situation triggered in her.

Limits About Me In This Situation

- I do not offer any benefit of the doubt to the nature of his schedule changes.

Practice 3: Fight For Gratitude

- I resent his assumption that I'm available.

- I interpret the situation as he is disrespecting me.

- I always say I'm available, even when I have important plans.

Now that the limits in both Michelle and her person have been identified, let's jump into the blessings. Blessings, like limits, are simply facts about good things. Your feelings about the blessings are not required for this exercise. Blessings about your former spouse may initially be understandably hard to uncover. It's ok to sit with it for a while. Michelle was ultimately able to make this list of her persons' blessings around the child sharing and scheduling issue:

Blessings About My Former Spouse In This Situation

- He feels free to talk to me about the custody schedule.

- Some part of him wants time with our kids and he is sure to schedule it.

- He contacts me when he can't keep his commitment.

- When he can't keep his commitment, he doesn't leave them with a girlfriend or his mom.

Simple and factual blessings. Don't fake these blessings. Don't write something down just to get it on the list. Write only what you can truly appreciate.

Notice it wasn't that he talks to her about the custody schedule, *and she knows it's a total joke.* It wasn't some part of him wants time with kids, *but he's totally lying because he never does.* It's not that he contacts her when he can't keep his commitment *like a total jerk.* The emotional feeling part

129

of your assessment is not necessary here; stick to the facts. As I said, if finding the blessings is hard for you initially, you are on the right path.

Now turn it on yourself again. Look at what blessings *you* bring or what blessings might emerge for *you* or in *you* with the situation as it is. For Michelle, she found quite a few.

Blessings About Me/For Me In This Situation

- I get to be the available parent for my kids.

- When his schedule changes, he leaves them with me, and I get more time with the kids.

- I'm letting my kids know one parent is always there for them.

- I may need help with schedule changes one day too, and this banks some goodwill toward that ask.

- I love showing up for my kids.

This last section can get tricky because we don't want our person's bad behavior to get them off the hook so easily. If I acknowledge that his failure to keep to the schedule has some payoff for me, then it feels like I'm condoning the behavior. You're not.

A few years back, my girlfriend's daughter turned ten, and her big birthday gift was that she would get her own bedroom. She would no longer share space with her annoying eight-year-old sister. She would have her own room all to herself. The day came to make the transition into the new room, and she was elated. She was free! But her enthusiasm was short lived. As she started moving her belongings into her new space, she realized that by her moving into *her* own room, she was now allowing her sister to also have *her* own room. In her mind, it wasn't fair for

Practice 3: Fight For Gratitude

her sister to benefit in this way. She was supposed to be getting the good thing; her sister should not get the good thing too.

We do the same thing in divorce recovery. We want our situation to improve, and we want our former partner's situation to suffer. Here is a hard truth: when you get better, everyone in your family gets the benefit, including your former spouse.

Limits and blessings are your starting place to improve your situation. The next step is to blend them into reality. We call this your person's limits and blessings reality. It takes both of your limits and blessings lists and merges them together into reality. It's a formula.

Limits + Blessings = Your Reality With Your Person

In Michelle's case, the formula started like this:

Limit: My person struggles to keep our schedule in its original form.

Blessing: I love that when the schedule changes it means I get more time with the kids.

Reality: I get a lot more time with my kids because my person sometimes struggles to keep our schedule as planned.

Story I Drop: He is using me to watch these kids and taking advantage of me.

New Story: I can work with this, and I willingly choose to do so in a way that supports my values.

But what about the fact that he's so inconsiderate and rude and takes advantage of her availability? Good question! What about it? It's not changing. She can trust that her person in this case will be inconsiderate and rude. He will be last minute. He will change things regularly. You know what? That is likely to never change. As Michelle would admit, this was often the way her person was when they were married. Your person doesn't change; if they do, it is rarely because of your suggestions.

People who struggle in an ongoing way with their divorce posture and recovery are still trying subconsciously to change their person. It's an unfortunate habit in both marriage and divorce, and it's a terrible way to love someone. And yet, we still return to this behavior and live with the frustrating results. Arguing with reality is exhausting. Working with reality can be a lot easier. If that's true, why are we all still taking the more exhausting route?

We do so because working with reality requires we take a close look at the blessings. People getting divorced, and sometimes years past it, are skilled in spotting the limits. The limits are more than ready for listing. When you start getting into the blessings, you lose a little something. That little something you lose is called your ego, or your story.

Your ego story serves a very important role for you. It is designed and maintained in an effort to protect you. This is good. It wants you to feel safe and justified and different from the others. Unfortunately, it also wants to keep you attached to the past. Your unchecked divorcing ego story wants you to be the victim and/or the hero of the story. It wants your person to be the perpetrator and/or the villain of the story. It wants you to be the victor! This is vindicating! It generates sympathy from your friends! It may make you hope that your kids will love you more because they see you're suffering from his garbage so much!

What are you without this story? It's not as scandalous then, is it? It's not as treacherous, and you're not so special. When you introduce blessings and gratitudes, your blustery story reads a little less exciting. Now you're no longer the victim. Now you're choosing to work with what is.

Practice 3: Fight For Gratitude

Michelle and I took it one level deeper into the "He never says he is sorry or expresses regret over the schedule changes" topic. Michelle set up the basic formula:

Limits About My Former Spouse In This Situation

- He doesn't say sorry when he inconveniences me.

- He acts like my schedule doesn't matter and is less important than his.

- He never apologizes for anything.

- He doesn't see how he contributes to our relationship being hard.

- He doesn't see the impact he's having on our kids.

Rough stuff. It's hard, really hard, being in relationship with an unapologetic person who lacks self-awareness.

Limits About Me In This Situation

- I can't seem to just do what needs to be done happily without this apology coming forth.

- I play the victim to his actions.

- I cannot keep my cool internally when he acts so casually and without regret.

Then we moved on to the blessings.

Blessings About My Former Spouse In This Situation

- His lack of apology leaves me open space to decide who I'm really doing this for—him, me, or the kids.

- He doesn't apologize in part because he relies on me with these kids.

The Best Worst Time of Your Life

- He relies on me because he knows I'm a rock for these kids.

- He doesn't engage with my frustration.

Blessing About Me In This Situation

- I'm deeply committed to my kids.

- I see the impact these last-minute changes and lack of regret are having on my kids.

- I'm not willing to let my kids suffer in order to prove a point to my person.

- I'm a great story narrator. I am great at shaping what happened into something they can understand.

Pull the formula together.

Limit: My person will not apologize when the schedule changes.

Blessing: I love that my motivation to do well for my kids comes from my own set of values and not someone else's actions or inactions.

Reality: His actions don't drive whether I live from my values. I choose to be there for my kids regardless of his actions.

Story I Drop: He is a selfish demanding rude man who takes advantage of my schedule and shows no remorse.

New Story: I can work with this, and I willingly choose to do so in a way that supports my values.

With this formula, you stop being stuck in "if he would just" and "I don't know why I am surprised because he always/never" world. You move into "I can work with this." It's not that it's over or easy or solved. It's just in play now. It's a moveable piece that just got put back in *your* court, where *you* can work with it. And just like the little ten-year-old girl who gave her sister a room to herself when she got one, you will end up giving good things to your former partner in the process. That's not our motivation though. Our motivation is getting unhooked, learning what to trust, and understanding what we want and are willing to give.

Long term relationship health generates from the perception of the relationship that exists within each individual. How you interpret situations dictates how you behave in them. The more you invest in a balanced relationship that focuses not only on the parts that are insufferable, but also the strengths, you will inch your partnership with your former spouse closer to success. It is the subtleties in our communication patterns that hurt the relationship over time. Working this practice puts you in a place to examine those subtleties that you're delivering and gives you a chance to redirect.

Admittedly, you may not want to see the full reality of life with your person. You will learn, however, as I did, that the universe thinks your "no" or your resistance to reality is adorable. That's our next practice. If it is helpful to you to keep your "no" close for now, be my guest. A gratitude practice coupled with this reflective formula helps you start to say a very soft yes. Not yes I want this, but yes I am willing to be shaped and remade. I am willing to learn to say yes to a life I didn't expect and let my former partner no longer hold center stage in the choices I make for myself or my kids.

LEARNING YOUR FORMER PARTNER'S OPERATING SYSTEM

Every person has an operating system. It's the hardwired equipment that fuels our daily activities and behaviors in life. The first pieces of your operating system were installed in your childhood and the system continues to be shaped in an ongoing way as you grow up and encounter new people, new situations, and new traumas. It is a fixed system in those for whom self-awareness is not a regular pursuit. It can be re-programmed in those who pursue it wholeheartedly.

To strengthen the Commitment arm of your Divorce Triangle you don't need to get to know your *own* operating system (do that in the Passion arm); I trust you're working on and growing in that already. Instead, resolve to become the technical expert and manager of your *former spouse's* operating system.

I am a technical expert in Mr. H's operating system. With regard to our overlapping lives, I know what delights him, what annoys him, what he will forget, and what he will and will not pay attention to. I know what makes him feel threatened, and I am familiar with how he relates to time. I know what comments from me trigger reactions in him, and I know where he struggles to be at his best. I know about his childhood and the patterns he lives out today as a result. I know what he excels at and what he counts on me to handle. I'm certain he knows the same for me.

Sounds like marriage doesn't it?! This resolution draws on the very same principles as marital harmony. Why? Your well-lived divorce will always draw on time proven marriage truths. Those truths are rooted in empathy, respect, and kindness. In your divorce, you don't get away from this person. You do a massive disentangling of your togetherness and then you keep at it. This rearranged relationship still needs most of what your marriage needed too.

If you took half an hour today, you could probably write up the technical specifications of your former spouse's operating system. Write it up. When you write it, you get distance from it.

Practice 3: Fight For Gratitude

It becomes the system that it is and probably always will be. It reminds you again of who you are dealing with. It shows you that the person you were married to still has a lot of the same characteristics of the one from whom you are now divorced. It may even generate some compassion, particularly as it relates to the childhood impacts your former spouse carries around.

After you become the technical expert of their operating system, the real work comes from learning how to become the manager of it. You can't *change* their operating system, only they can. Drop the insights you have for them about how to do better. Focus instead on getting yourself in a place to *manage* it. You manage it by protecting yourself and by learning the new skills necessary to do so well.

To manage my former partner's operating system, I have worked to accept what it is and what it can't be. I have learned new communication styles that protect me from small and big irritations with him. I have a map for how his operating system triggers my hot buttons, and I have a plan for how to settle those triggers once flipped. I know how to help him feel safe. I work on what our future together looks like. I learned how to translate my hostility into words that support my greater goals.

You can do this too. Gratitude is what you need to start shifting the story.

QUESTIONS FOR YOUR DEEPENING

1. Are you open to undertaking a gratitude practice for your former partner? Why or why not?

2. Identify a troublesome divorce situation you're dealing with at the moment. Submit it to the Limits + Blessings = Your Reality with Your Person formula. What did you learn?

3. Write up the technical specifications of your former spouse's operating system. What delights them, what annoys them, what they will forget, and what they will and will not pay attention to? What makes them feel threatened, how do they relate to time, what comments from you trigger reactions in them, where do they struggle to be at their best? What did they experience in childhood and what patterns do they live out today as a result?

Chapter 8

Practice 4: Say Yes

After Mr. H's Proclamation of Disconnection, I did the only thing I knew to do well. I said no. I said it a lot. As I said no, I took a ride on the "about to be a divorced woman" carousel. It's a classic ride. I lost weight. I saw a counselor. I thought of all of the ways that this was his fault. I reviewed every season of our life together and wondered if it was truly happy or just imagined. I anticipated every future moment and assured myself that each one would be awful. I prayed. I screamed. I took long walks. I talked my friends' ears off. I stopped sleeping. I started working. I stopped eating. I started drinking. I stopped drinking. I started running. I tripped and fell while running. All the while, I was hanging on to my "no" like it was my security blanket.

No. I do not want to break my children's hearts by telling them this news.

No. I do not want to miss half of my children's lives.

No. I do not want to sit alone in my home during my holidays without them.

No. I do not want to live with the humiliation of being a divorcée.

139

No. I don't like this, and I don't want this.

No. My future will be miserable.

Daniel Gilbert, a Harvard professor, psychologist, and author of *Stumbling on Happiness*, has done some fascinating research on how we humans tend to look at our future lives. He and his team worked with close to 20,000 people and found one major takeaway: people are not good at predicting how they will feel in the future after things don't go their way. In fact, they really stink at it. He noticed that when assessing where things are going to go from where we are right now, we predict that things will basically never change. It's weird isn't it? We naturally think this is the end of what it is.

This is awesome to hear if you're on top of the world and a little devastating if you're at rock bottom.

What this means for those divorcing is that we do very poorly at guessing what our emotions in our future will feel like. We look at the future and focus in on one or two details of that picture, while failing to realize just how many other factors will come to bear on it. For example, when I was picturing my future divorced life, the two factors I used to predict my future happiness were the fact that I wouldn't see my kids all of the time and I would never love a man ever again. I would suffer through terrible weekends without them. I would live alone and be single and sad. This was what I knew, and this was what my emotions told me was the future I would inhabit. It was a future with no future.

Meanwhile, people I knew who were divorced assured me I would need those breaks from the girls, especially if I was raising them as the only adult in our home. They told me that I would absolutely fall in love again. I, in my seeming wisdom at the

Practice 4: Say Yes

time, told them they were dead wrong. No, you don't know me, I'll be crushed every time they are gone. I wouldn't dare to love again; men are more work than they are worth.

What I couldn't see, though, was the *person* I would become while living in these circumstances. I saw myself in a static place: super sad, super tired, closed off from love, profoundly afraid, and trying to be accepting. And in my mind, I presumed that I would forever live in this place. I could receive no reassurance from anyone that it would be any different. I had never been divorced, and so if this is how it feels right now, then this is what I need to get used to.

What I couldn't see were the many *other* factors that would play a part in my growth that I had not even considered. The new people I would meet who would cause me to think differently, the ways my new job would change my confidence, the way my weight loss process would affect my perspective on what it meant to love myself and to engage with men, the ways my children were growing and integrating our new family rhythms. I could only see what was right in front of me.

It's funny looking back now. My girls and I have talked about how we enjoy close and supportive relationships, and we credit our time away from each other on Dad's weekends to that reality. We get a breather, we miss each other, and we return making sure our time together is dear to us. The thing I dreaded most just might be the thing that is getting us through the teenage years with solid footing. As far as being single, I decided early on that I wouldn't be a good mother for other people's children. I didn't want the distraction from my own kids, and it wasn't for me. Lo and behold, the dearest single man would enter my life. He was 45 years old, never married and had no kids. Within weeks, love snuck up on me and I was thinking about what our

141

The Best Worst Time of Your Life

lives might look like together. He took my single life and made it coupled. We got married, and the structure of our new family looks wildly different than I ever thought it would.

So, on both factors—weekends without kids and a loveless future—my divorcing friends got it right. They predicted I would need those breaks. Of course, at first when I was dealing with these issues, it upended my world and I struggled so much to get familiar in my own life for days without them. Where my married friends were craving a break like I had, I couldn't enjoy the one I was given. For years—yes years—it was really hard. But now, it's fine. I'm fine most of the time. They're fine most of the time. The spaces in our togetherness as mother and daughters gets some relief from our times away. My friends also predicted I would fall in love again. They were right. I didn't even try to resist it when it arrived. My sense of comfort in these two factors is far different than I predicted it would be at the outset.

How could this be?

I'm the one actually living my life, and yet I'm the one who gets it wrong?

I'm just like the people Dr. Gilbert studied, and so are you. His research revealed that when asked about their future ten years from now, people would anticipate that they would change very little. Those same people, consulted ten years later, instead reported a tremendous amount of growth and change in themselves. This happened at all decades of life. We are simply terrible at predicting who we think we will be in relationship to our future situations.

What does that mean for us on the front end of an unknown and possibly dreaded future like the one divorce produces? How do we imagine ourselves into something better than what our initial instincts will produce and thereby relieve a little of the despair that we see it in?

Practice 4: Say Yes

It's not just positive thinking. If you force yourself to think unbelievable thoughts too quickly, you set yourself up for failure. The answer is actually a bit unexpected: Gilbert suggests we look to other people. If you're like me, you don't like taking other people's experiences and putting them with your own. You think you are terribly unique, and you want to experience things for yourself and believe that everything you are going through no one has ever been through in this exact way with these exact circumstances. If this is true, then what could someone else's experience possibly have to say about mine?

As it turns out, quite a bit. The truth that Gilbert uncovered was that our ability to predict how we will do in a situation is much better informed by listening to someone else's experience rather than insisting on our own first-person experience. We are more than happy to trust other people with restaurant and product reviews, movie recommendations, and where to go on vacation, but we draw the line at our really personal stuff. No one could possibly relate to that. We think that we wouldn't dare lean on someone else's experience.

DON'T GO IT ALONE

This, my friends, is our downfall. When we insist on going it alone, carving out our own very painful "you don't get me and this is like nothing else ever before" space, we imagine a future for ourselves where there are very few alternatives to the sad way forward we envision. Our claims to having the alcoholic husband, the narcissist husband, the checked-out husband, the mentally unstable husband, the traveling husband, the poor husband, the vindictive husband, the cheater husband... they are what give us our supposed uniqueness and beloved storyline. When we claim we have the critical wife, the withholding wife, the emotionally difficult wife...that is what we cling to when it

143

gets dark. Of course no one understands, we conclude, they don't have a "fill in the blank" husband or wife.

I'm not saying that these types of husbands and wives aren't hard to be getting divorced from! They are terribly difficult! It's true, not everyone will understand. There are people who actually *do* understand. Even if they don't meet your threshold for *really* understanding, they do know that who you are now with this "fill in the blank" husband or wife is not who you are going to be three months from now. They know that you will learn. You will experiment. You will grow. What it means to live with whatever majorly difficult, burdensome, tricky, complicated, high conflict mess you are in right now is not a permanent place. When we silo ourselves off, we can't imagine for ourselves that we would ever be in a meaningful process of maturation, of rising to our moment, of leveling up our behaviors, of opening to all kinds of new ways of living.

Our fourth practice of saying yes is to know that "sure" is not a four-letter word. Our first meek practice of "sure" in this case is to utter, "Sure, I want to hear your story." It's leaning on the sisterhood or brotherhood of those who have divorced before you. You lean on them not because you will end up as they did, but because you are now going to follow a path with only a few really important turns on it. You will be shocked, you will grieve, you will deal with a tremendous number of logistics, you will face profoundly difficult thoughts about this person you used to love, you will realize what you are losing, you will figure out housing, custody schedules, and asset divisions, you will buy things and sell things, you will tweak your career, face a few new traditions in your holidays, possibly date someone, possibly marry someone and have days where your former partner who consumes your every thought actually doesn't come up in your brain for an entire day. We are very unique, our stories are

Practice 4: Say Yes

preciously unique, but we are also just all the same. Our survival and rebirth as divorced and ultimately single women and men follows known contours. Yes, your story is unique, but you are joining us. This club that no one wants to be qualified to join, well, you just got the membership letter. Once you are one of us, you too will know what lives behind the veil.

I compare it to the same veil that women share about child rearing. They tell you when you welcome a child home that you have no idea what kind of love this child will open in you. You see the dirty cars new moms have, they look tired, and they don't go out as much as they used to. And you think, my baby, my story, we're different. You don't know us. Once you enter motherhood, though, you realize that our survival and rebirth as mothers also follows known contours. Yes, your story is unique, but you are joining countless others. Once you are one of them, you too will know what lives behind the veil.

With fellow divorcées, when you listen to their stories, you don't need to spend a lot of time comparing spouses, children, finances, and gripes. Get to the richer spot. Ask the divorced and divorcing women and men you know important questions, the kind of questions that expose the contours and not the specifics. Ask them what they discovered about themselves that they did not know was there before the divorce. Divorced people you seek out will tell you that some new part of themselves emerged along the way, and that it that really surprised them. They will tell you of unexpected friendships and alliances that appeared once they were single. They will tell you of devastation that was anticipated that never came to be or came to be in ways that they could rise to address. They have stories of when they realized they were going to be OK. They survived. Ask them who stepped in in ways they didn't expect, and find out what made it easier for them.

We so quickly seek out advisors on the material elements of their story (the lawyer, the settlement, the cheating) and miss the bigger heart picture that we really desperately need to see. Because when you compare just these facts about your life—your address, your job, your medical condition, your in-laws, your family business—you will easily get in your silo and think you can't learn anything from this person. Their divorce is nothing like yours. But when you get a little deeper than the facts, when you get into the heart of their experience, that's the place where you most need to listen.

They are not your stories and of course we have no idea just what factors make your story complicated, but there are collective stories of divorce that you absolutely need to hear. You need to hear that you will get through this, because you will.

Let's move on to another practice of "sure" you will need to consider on the path.

As those of you on the receiving end of an unwanted divorce know, it takes two people to stay married and only one person to get a divorce. This is the most unfair negotiation. As those painful conversations with Mr. H ultimately got started, my head was forced to make future plans with him about life without him, while my heart was still yelling "no" at a deafening pitch.

I remember reading something during my darkest days of divorcing that said that those who are most successful with the process of divorce are those who act like they chose it. For those of us who are largely not in favor of the divorce we find ourselves in, this seems unlikely to happen. That concept has haunted me for years. How could I possibly act like I chose it?

146

Practice 4: Say Yes

HOW TO GET TO YES

Tara Brach was the first person to work on my "no." Brach is a teacher of meditation, emotional healing and spiritual awakening, as well as a psychologist. I highly recommend her guided meditations as you seek to calm your own storm within. In one of her meditations and in her book, *Radical Acceptance: Embracing Your Life with the Heart of a Buddha*, she warns that "The boundary to what we can accept is the boundary to our freedom." She suggests that if we can accept our reality as it comes to us, then we will have no limits on our experience of freedom. Our limits are found where our "no" begins.

I was definitely at a limit. I had a hard no. Acceptance of reality? No. It felt powerless and pathetic. It felt like giving up. It felt weak and uncommitted. I saw myself as a fighter, as though there was no fight I wouldn't enter. Even my marriage therapist encouraged me when he said that I fought like heck for what mattered to me. I told myself that I would fight for *my* reality, not the reality I was presented with.

I walked the line alternating between a strong "no" and a somewhat mild "no" for nine years. During the majority of these nine years, the "no" did not feel like an optional response. How would I say "yes" to our family not being together? How would I agree and align with a breakup that had so very many ripples and complications, many of which I still had to contend with? Why would I want to say "yes" to the failure of my marriage? What was the point of saying "yes" to a situation that was very clearly weighing heavy on the hearts of my children? The "yes" seemed reckless, heartless even. To say "yes" felt like a betrayal of everything I hold dear to. My "no" was my anchor.

147

"Yes" felt like a heavy coat in a Phoenix summer: ill-fitting and not necessary. More than that, "yes" felt like I was giving a pass to Mr. H for the hurt. Saying "yes" to my reality was letting him win, and I was not about to let that happen. My "no" would be a billboard to him that what happened was not acceptable. If I said "yes," he would get away with this.

I have a friend, Liz, who I fortuitously met when I was pregnant with my first child. Six months ahead of me on the parenting journey, she had a magical Mary Poppins effect on my daughter. Pool dates, play dates, mall trips, and early morning breakfasts with strollers made up our time together in those early years. You can't spend more than a day with Liz and not notice that her world is tilted in the direction of yes. She says "sure." She says it a lot. Where I can have a no posted on my heart's front door, hers is wide open and welcoming. I don't say sure. I think, "Um, maybe let me think about it, it's tricky, it involves sacrifice, I might not get what I want, this is definitely not what I need, inconvenience is buried in this, what will we eat, I'm tired." After I think that, I say "no." After that, I might say "sure," but it's often reluctant.

Liz doesn't suffer from the thoughts before the sure comes out. I've asked her about this, and she says it comes from her connection with the greater good. She's more certain that moving through the chaos and discomfort that "sure" carries with it will ultimately lead to connection. She feels stuck and stagnant at "no"; "yes" takes her to adventure and the part of the story that's waiting to be told. She understands that she also needs to say yes to herself for those exact same reasons.

My life lived against Liz's mirror has illustrated Brach's point that you can't say yes until you see all of the ways that you say no. Wow, I said no a lot. I said no to just about everything that wasn't my idea. I had, still have, lots of enjoyment around

Practice 4: Say Yes

the idea of control. Throw a divorce into the heart of a woman who loves control and you've got major conflict brewing. My resistance was in force.

We know that pain times resistance equals suffering. My pain was inevitable. My resistance was learned and it was in fact something within my control. My suffering was really a product of my own making. The pain was something to be sat in, allowed, permitted. As I resisted the pain, I created the suffering–the ruminating, shallow, twisted against-ness that would ultimately limit my freedom.

My no was the limit of my freedom. How would I learn to say sure?

Brach explains that our yes doesn't mean we feel great about what is happening. It doesn't mean we advocate for it and treasure it. Our yes is simply an acknowledgement of the moment we find ourselves in. And it unlocks us to act in the next moment with greater intention. She says our yes is courageous, where our no holds us back. Yes is possible, no is reactive. As we walk through our divorce, when we resist the pain, when we push against and say no, what we are really resisting is the loss.

All of my small "no"s could be wrapped up into one big no: no, I don't want to lose this familiar life I know. I don't know what divorced life looks like, what holidays look like in this arrangement, what home I will live in, what job I will have, what finances will support me. I don't know what Friday nights look like and I'm not sure if love will ever find a home in me again. Losing everything was destabilizing, and it animated the biggest no I held. I couldn't see how to build up the Intimacy leg of my Divorce Triangle, meaning I couldn't see how to engage the relationship in new ways. I could only see how the old ways were fading away.

149

Had I continued in my defiant no, I would have ended up as one of those women—you know the type. They are the ones who get described first by their divorced status. The ones who talk about their former spouses in ways that make everyone uncomfortable. The ones who regret ever having entered their relationship. Victims. Cynical. Robbed. Defeated. I didn't yet know who I wanted to be, but I was sure who I didn't want to be. I didn't want to be that woman.

We have already established that walking your heart with care through this process is unbelievably difficult. To end up in a place where your heart can radiate the kind of grace and love that builds a very good post-divorce life requires a great deal of work, as we covered in the three preceding practices, but inhabiting it also requires a willingness. It requires a willingness to say yes to the life you did not and would not choose. That yes is bigger than any no you've been nursing.

THE OTHER WOMAN

Cue the other woman. Her relationship with my husband ate me up. She showed up at a difficult time in our struggle, and logically, I began with "no." No, you may not have access to my husband, no you may not have access to my children, and no you may not enter my life. She hit on every trigger point David Rock outlines in his S.C.A.R.F. model which identifies a specific trigger category to encompass generally all threats. She triggered my Status as a mother, feeling as though I might be replaced, or her fun factor might exceed mine. My Certainty was triggered as another adult with her own ways of living intersected with mine and I wasn't sure what parts of life would need to shift as a result. My Autonomy was threatened, because now I was not only thinking through what Mr. H needed or wanted, I had to anticipate how those decisions would impact her as well. My

Practice 4: Say Yes

sense of Relatedness was crushed. I didn't feel part of the group and wasn't sure how we could possibly become "family" under these circumstances. And Fairness. Well, that was triggered off the charts. This was definitely unfair.

Thus began a very intense, prolonged, and honest period of emotional upheaval. Letters were written. Dark nights of the soul were experienced. Hurt like nothing I had ever felt before seemed to be stuck on me. My "no" knew it was being given a warning. It couldn't persist with all of these new relationship combinations in play.

I took several important steps to get to my "yes" around this new addition. Had I known these were the steps I was taking, it would have made it a much easier path. I was blind at the time, but in hindsight, I can offer you these recommendations:

First, acknowledge that you are at different points in the divorce process than your former spouse. As we saw in the chart in Chapter 4, the mental and emotional transition through the change of divorce follows a largely similar path for everyone through denial, anger, confusion, frustration, stress and then onto impatience, and ultimately, hope and energy. However, some will compress that path and finish it quickly; others will take years to make progress. Some will walk the path so privately you'll think they skipped over it; others will take so long you wonder if they will ever get themselves back together. The thing to understand is that you are *never* in the same recovery spot as your former partner. Your downfall will be to think that you are. Your former partner is acting like this because they are not in the same spot that you are. When you can release them to be where they are, you can invest more energy into working with the priorities of where *you* are in your own recovery.

151

I wish I knew about this and the fact that Mr. H was much further along the divorce recovery path than I was. He was in the New Beginnings section. I was in the Endings section. When your Endings collides with someone else's New Beginnings, you have a lot of conflict. Knowing this can give everyone in the process a lot more grace to operate.

My second recommendation is to resolve to be the bigger person. The temptation is to be small: to vilify the new woman, to reduce your former partner, and to let everyone know just how wrong this is...often. I surely did. Instead, use caution and save it only for a select audience. Most days, strive to rise above. Seek to disentangle yourself from their story and invest in your own. Agree to let this happen. Let your partner get away with it (they will anyway). Commit to being the most beautiful person you can be in it.

Create an intention to contribute to your part of either a great marriage or a great divorce. Make these the only two options. Give yourself these guardrails.

Third, get off their social media. Now. Unfollow your former partner and don't look the other woman up. Tell your friends to not give you updates either. Knowing what they are up to only leads to further anger and despair and isn't an act of kindness to yourself. Speaker and author Byron Katie talks about the concept of your business, their business, and God's business. This new relationship is their business and God's business. It is not your business. And that is the hardest part of all, because for years, maybe decades, your partner's business *was* your business. Leaving them to their own business is a critical step in divorce recovery. Give your heart a wide berth to heal; don't invite reminders of what they are up to with each other.

Practice 4: Say Yes

Diving into the details of Mr. H's life with her was my heart's attempt at figuring out why this happened. It was an expedition to understand the story. If I could figure that out, I reasoned, this wouldn't hurt so badly. Wrong. It hurt worse. The answer wasn't on Facebook.

Lastly, carve out where this new person intersects with your life and figure out how to work with that. I kept saying, "But she's with my kids now!" I didn't like that fact, but there weren't true threats to my children's health and safety at stake. She was going to spend time with my kids. This part *was* my business. Working through expectations, boundaries, and general protocols was part of being the bigger person and demonstrating that I was willing work with this inevitable and unwanted twist in my story. We got together and she committed to me that she would never want to take my role as mom. She wasn't going to compete. I told her to never take the girls to get their hair cut. It was a feeble first step.

More than any of these steps to growing my "sure" to its greatest potential, I had to nurture the new thought that love gets bigger, not halved. I mistakenly thought that by allowing her to be in our lives, I would have to share some part of the love my kids and I enjoyed with her. That wasn't the case for me, and it won't be the case for you. Love is not finite. It is expansive and never-ending. As mothers, we know how much we love our first kid and worry we won't have enough love to fit in another kid and yet love gets bigger. It will get bigger for you and for your kids as you welcome new members of your family.

FORGIVENESS

As we approach the end of this book, I know that at least a few of you have noticed that the concept of forgiveness has not

The Best Worst Time of Your Life

been addressed. Forgiveness is a tricky topic for me. I certainly would be standing first in line to tout its importance. I'm also aware that it gets used in some lightweight ways that I wouldn't support, and I don't think are helpful for your real, true, and beautiful divorce recovery.

I've noticed in my work with divorcing women that many of them throw around the concept of forgiveness rather lightly. They say, "Yeah, I just forgave him and moved on." Meanwhile their destructive comments about their former partner don't match that sentiment in the least. I get it. You do feel a little pressured to forgive when you're divorced. It makes other people happy to hear you've forgiven the other person. It makes *you* happy to hear that you've forgiven them. You want to forgive, you realize it's healing, and you say it. You say, "I forgive you." You think, "I really hate you still a little bit, but I hate you less than a few months ago, and overall I forgive you." You said it; therefore, you believe it is real.

I tried that. For many years my working definition of forgiveness was letting Mr. H get away with it. It wasn't noble, but it was honest. I said, "I'm letting you get away with doing what you're doing and I'm not going to stand in your way." I was wrestling with not wanting him to have the satisfaction of seeing me live a great life post-divorce. I felt that if I lived my life well without him, then that evidence would somehow let him off the hook. He'd congratulate himself for doing the right thing.

Some of you don't even think about forgiving your former spouse. You're waiting for the *real* "I'm sorry" from them to even start thinking about it. You wouldn't dare forgive someone who doesn't apologize. You want some grand statement from them where they see their faults and own how they contributed to this mess. You want them to say (and feel) really, *really* sorry. This is a fair spot to occupy for a while. You want the adult version of

154

Practice 4: Say Yes

the preschool playground supervisor to walk them over to you and make them say they are sorry so you can say I forgive you.

I'll let you in on a secret. I got a version of that "I'm truly sorry" confession. I got it a few times. Mr. H definitely owned his part, and to his credit, he humbled himself to say it to me. Do you know what surprised me though? It didn't matter. I didn't need it. In fact, his sorry didn't really even move anything in me because his sorry was remarkably powerless in my life. Of course, I appreciated it, but at the end of the day, it didn't change me. His sorry didn't put us back together, it didn't relieve the kids of pain, and it didn't make me less angry. I started to ask myself then, how sorry would he have to be before it starts to make a difference for me? I couldn't find a metric that would measure what I thought I needed.

When it comes to truly healing from divorce, you can certainly start with the concept of forgiveness. Come up with your own definition; use mine if it fits. Start contemplating what it would mean to offer forgiveness. Just beware that stopping there is incomplete. Offering forgiveness doesn't do the hard work of getting your own heart in a place to offer reconciliation.

Where forgiveness releases the wrong and no longer seeks to hold the other person accountable for their many missteps, reconciliation seeks to restore the relationship. True reconciliation involves both parties coming together and both wanting to find a new way forward. Most divorced couples will never reconcile. One party may be interested, but reconciliation takes willingness from two parties. Even though your relationship with your former spouse may never be reconciled, it is imperative that you train your heart to offer your side of that reconciliation effort. You do it not because your former partner deserves it. You do it because you deserve it.

In his book *The Peacemaker*, Ken Sande lays out four commitments we can make as we offer true and abiding forgiveness:

1. I will not dwell on this incident.

2. I will not bring this incident up and use it against you.

3. I will not talk to others about this incident.

4. I will not allow this incident to stand between us or hinder our personal relationship.

For those divorcing, these are gigantic promises. We may not even get to genuinely live from them in their entirety. I know I didn't follow them 100% of the time. But what would happen if we took these steps in order and let them reside in us and expand in us over time?

If you stopped dwelling on the divorce, his stonewalling, her cheating, or his anger, what might have room to grow in your thoughts instead? Could you start to live into your own single life? Could you focus on what comes next for you? Could you make plans to develop your own interests and commitments?

This is the biggest "yes" of all. If you stopped bringing up his inconsistencies, her unreliability, and his lying and using it against him, what could you bring up instead? Could you allow your former partner to exist unchanged while you develop communication and coping skills that address your reality with them? If you stopped talking to others about her selfishness, his girlfriend, and her constant schedule changing, what could you talk about instead? Could you talk about how you're so proud of the way you're handling this?

The last commitment Sande outlines—I won't let it stand it the way of our relationship—is a tough one to handle early on.

156

Practice 4: Say Yes

This commitment is an overflow of the good footing you gain and the progress you make in addressing the first three. This one emerges from your well-trained heart over time.

As pastor and author Meghan Good says, "Forgiveness doesn't require warm feelings, it is the release of the other person back into the hands of God." It is saying "This person means more to God than they do to me. Their story must be untangled by someone wiser than me. I am not God." Insert Creator, Spirit, or Essence for God here and you've got a humbling and deeply freeing posture to take. It's not up to you to fix them. It never was.

There is no sorry from your former partner that will release the pain you carry. It might help, but it's not the answer you should seek. Tracking down the real story and finding out why it happened also won't get you very far. Neither will blame, nor will a thin level forgiveness statement. Judy Hahn says, "The grace is to walk away from the why." When we let go of the "why," we can better inhabit the now. The now is the only place from which we can start practicing the four commitments of forgiveness and let a truly new chapter of the story be told that starts with a "sure."

Sure is not a four letter word in the classic sense. The sure you offer by saying yes to a life you didn't choose helps you start to offer a committed level of intentional forgiveness. It invites the adventure my friend Liz hinted at. There's a story beyond your no, and it's a story you actually are in charge of. It's not dictated by circumstances, it's created by you. Pull out a journal and start laying out all of your "no"s. Is there a small yes you can start to work with?

QUESTIONS FOR YOUR DEEPENING

1. Reach out to another person who has gone through divorce. Ask him or her: what aspect of yourself did you discover that you didn't know was there before the divorce? Who stepped in in ways you didn't expect?

2. Where is your "no" limiting what you can welcome in your post-divorce life? Where are you being invited to say "yes" to a life you didn't expect?

3. What is your starter definition for forgiveness as it relates to your divorce?

Chapter 9

What Remains

Out of the blue one day when my youngest was in elementary school, she asked me a question I'll never forget. "Mom, how many husbands will you have?"

From the Proclamation of Disconnection to signed papers approved by the court, my divorcing process lasted about four years. A couple years after that, I married another man who was happy to inherit our story, contribute good things to it, be a friend to my first husband, and be a stable and loving step-father for my kids. We live about 10 minutes away from Mr. H and we spend holidays, birthdays, and other important moments as a tribe.

Her question made me crack up laughing.

Me! The do-gooder, A+ student, who prides herself on being upright and honorable! I just got asked how many husbands I was going to have. This is not the impression I wanted my daughter to have of me.

So, I answered her honestly.

"I thought I'd have one husband, and I have two husbands. So now I think I'll only have two, so I'll probably have three."

This comeback wasn't to hint at some future break up with my current husband, it was the culmination of a decade of inner work. It was me (me!) with an openness to unexpected turns in the road. It was me owning my story that I'm a woman with a couple of husbands, and I'm fully capable of handling what comes down the pike next. It was me with a "sure" at the ready.

Let me return to that other statement I just made—the one about living about 10 minutes away from Mr. H and spending holidays, birthdays, and other important moments together as a family. We divorced over a period of four years. I've been recovering for those four years plus another six years. I've worked very hard for the freedom I now enjoy. Let's not skip over that.

In every single case, it was an unexpected and difficult time that precipitated my deeper growth and that led to the life I enjoy with a full heart today. Oh, how I wish I could have grown in the easy times, but it was rarely that way. Mr. H and his girlfriend eventually broke up. It was devastating for all of us in different ways. He lost a partner. The girls lost a beloved adult in their lives. I lost the person I had learned to welcome into our lives through an enormously difficult growth process. I was petrified to see who would be next. I've spent listless weekends without the girls wondering what life is supposed to look like when they are absent. It seems like the lights are on at our home when they are here and then they flicker out when they go to their other home. I've been disappointed and frustrated more times than I can count at how the logistics of a bi-nuclear home play out in real time. From lost pants to missed appointments to the really big heart issues of life, it has pulled at everything in me.

I sought out more spiritual direction, did a juice fast, got a colonic, and found support from a naturopath. I would do all of it again. Each piece built on the other even though it felt like I was grabbing at straws.

Then 2019 came. I'd started writing this book in earnest for you, and it hit me that year that I didn't have the deep abiding victory in my heart that I wanted to inspire you to go after. A decade after the whole thing started falling apart, I was singularly focused on what it would take to be free of my own thoughts and wishing it could be different. I devoured books I had read many years before and dug deeper than ever to find the answer. The "aha!" came for me in one quote from author and speaker Paula D'Arcy. D'Arcy speaks with authority in the pain department having lost her husband and young daughter in an automobile accident that she survived while pregnant. She went on to deliver their unborn child and bring a message of yes to the world through her teachings and writings.

She talked about agreeing to the terms of life and all of its moving parts, and it hit me like the invitation that it is. After nearly a decade of pursuit, I was ready to agree to the terms of life and the inescapable change that it would include. Instead of saying, "It shouldn't be this way," I was able to work with the sentence, "Sure, it could be this way." Which turned into, "Yes, I'll allow it this way." That led to "If it is this way, how do I live into it with the best of everything in me?" And the life that came with aligning myself with the way it will be even if I didn't want it became a surprisingly very good life.

LITTLE WINS ADD UP

In our pursuit of becoming better people who are more equipped to handle our lives, we will often point to one moment that we look back on as the day we washed our hands of something or felt released or moved on in some meaningful way. Just before Christmas 2019 was that day for me. But I'm aware and want you to be too that it wasn't that moment alone that created the freedom. That moment was built on millions of other moments that lead to the great release. We can't be looking for the one silver bullet of truth that will change it all for us. We need to keep showing up to the process of collecting and amassing small, incremental, hardly noticeable subtle truths over days, months, and years. We need to rehearse these four practices with consistency. It is on these collective truths that the big "aha!" can emerge.

Process has value to the extent that it leads us to one of the sweetest results: perspective. Perspective is a major factor in finding meaning. Perspective is defined as the "true understanding of the relative importance of things; a sense of proportion." Mine was born of time and pursuit and will alight upon you as well.

What keeps me going? I had an insistence that I can still become something greater, and a deeply held belief that divorce would not destroy my children or myself. I had a knowing, carved out over dark days and sleepless nights, that light always wants to win. I also knew that I could regulate out of the constant fight or flight of those early years.

What keeps me going is an abiding devotion to building and rebuilding my Divorce Triangle with each new struggle that presents itself. For Intimacy, I keep working at gratitude for Mr. H, finding ways to celebrate all that he brings to our post-divorce family. For Passion, I seek out self-growth as a mission of my soul and I work at developing my capacity to handle what this life looks like for us. For Commitment, I'm engaging and re-engaging the relationship I have with Mr. H in each new season. We may not be married, but we are in relationship. This Divorce Triangle is my bedrock. I hope for it to be yours too.

162

In her *Coventry: Essays* book, author Rachel Cusk lays out the hard reality of divorce. She writes, "The central shock of divorce lies in its bifurcation of the agreed-upon version of life: There are now two versions, mutually hostile, each of whose narrative aim is to discredit the other." That's the way it goes without your conscious effort. It's your story against your former partner's story. Your version—he stopped working at it, he cheated, and he ruined our family—sits alongside your partner's version—she can't accept me as I am, I'm tired of her unrealistic demands, and she never respected me. Your voice will get louder and louder as you try to insist on your narrative. Your ability to secure popular opinion toward your version is a deep need. When you're losing your life as you recognize it, you work to make very sure that you keep the narrative in your favor.

There will come a time when you too get an invitation to move past this marker. My narrative meant the world to me. When I looked more closely at it, though, it tied me to two things: my past and Mr. H. It ensured that I would always be identifying as divorced. Divorce is about the closing down of a marriage. With children, it's also about the rearranging of a family. By clinging to my narrative and my past, I couldn't give my present situation a shot at thriving. I was too occupied being divorced, still closing down, still fighting for justice, still wanting something that was no longer available to me.

The shift is a simple invitation. Do you want to be divorced? Or are you ready to be single? Or in my case, was I ready to give my whole heart to my new marriage? Would I live into my new relationship and not make him pay for the damage that was left from before? By allowing it to be as it would be, I was finally able to move from victim to creator. What did I want my life to be about now and going forward? Was I brave enough to leave the narrative and start a new one? Would I be able to be the gardener of my own soul, and work with the future hope that something beautiful was emerging?

TWO-ADDRESS FAMILY

A final note on the kids. Most kids want to be part of a family that is comfortable, full of good memories, and shepherded by adults who realize the formational aspects of the family system. I've watched a number of well-intentioned divorced parents do a fantastic job at creating this sense of family at their new home address with the kids. When the kids are with them, they give 100%, work hard at passing on important values, and do the work of parenting well. They make the memories, have the fun, and keep close tabs on the emotional states of their children.

This one-address family is something you will want to get right, but there's another invitation in front of you. It was extended to me as well, and it starts with the understanding that your kids want to be part of one family, not two separate families. They don't want to see their lives on two separate stages, occupying your family at your home and another family at their other parent's home. They want one family.

How do you do that for them? It starts with your intention to work toward the notion of a two-address family. Two-address families are defined by the ability of one parent to offer only one deeply important thing: the genuine, regular, heartfelt holding, shaping, and narration of the experience of divorced family life for your child. It is the ultimate parenting act for you to hold the story for them and help them see a different way of writing it. It is a careful undertaking to shape the sometimes difficult and unsavory elements of their other parent and weave a true and supportive story that invites your child to consider what love looks like in this situation. Being the narrator is a position of humble and great power. You hold in your hands the ability to spin a one-sided story with yourself as the hero, but you also have the raw material to start chapter one of the hero's journey for your own kid. This two-address family commitment may mean that you need to sacrifice the desire to close yourself off from their other parent's existence. It will stretch you to places you previously thought unimaginable.

Two-address families are able to offer to their children an experience of their other parent, even when that parent isn't there. "You got an A on your report card? I bet your dad would be so proud!" "You aren't sure about tryouts for the basketball team? Mom is great with helping you sort out those kinds of decisions." Two-address families can also reflect on the positive experiences of when they were a one-address family. "When you were a baby, your dad and I loved to argue over who would get to hold you out in public." "I remember when you were learning to walk your mom was always laughing at how your mouth hung open when you were working at it." Two-address families allow the other parent to occupy mental and heart space in the home, even when they don't sleep there.

You may have a long list of disappointments about your child's other parent, but your kid deserves to live in a good story and a good family. Family is what we make of it. Family celebrates the blessings that each person can bring, and it is able to tell a story about the struggles that exhibits compassion. As a two-address family parent, you can and should empathize with the struggles your child has with the other parent, but you can and should draw the line at commiserating. Our kids want our empathy; our commiseration makes them worry that things aren't ok. "Your dad was distracted all weekend? Oh sweetheart, I know how that hurts. Dad means well and it's hard for us adults to always get it right." "Your mom seemed angry when you were with her? That's a scary feeling, and I know you just want to feel

165

safe around both of us. When you're ready, I think we should talk about ways to do that." As parents, it is incumbent upon us to talk in ways that advance our child's safety and sense of wellbeing, not give voice to our vindictive, exasperated story of agreement. We work to build up, not pile on.

The two-address family parent knows the story, is comfortable in it, and narrates it to the kids in ways that create safety for them. The two-address family parent is one who the kids can trust to piece it together. Our kids look to us for direction. Let's make sure it's the kind of direction that leads to a destination we desire.

PIECING IT BACK TOGETHER

My hope is that these practices will be your companion as you start to think your way into new possibilities. Be very certain, though: your thinking will only get you so far. You will need to revisit the practices here and *live* your way into new realities. The brain can only aspire to the things you most want. It will take your daily commitment to show up with the best of you and offer it willingly to the process of recovery and building something beautiful.

My divorce coaching practice is built upon the concept of Kintsugi. Kintsugi is the Japanese art of repairing broken pottery. This practice involves using lacquer mixed with gold, silver, or platinum to repair the pieces. It treats the breakage and repair as a part of the rich history of an object, rather than trying to hide it. The repair is literally illuminated, revered, and treasured, reminding us that our difficult circumstances can be remade more beautiful than they were before. When carefully pieced together, we can bring about a new object, a new story, or a new life thread that wouldn't have been possible without the painful breaking. In doing so, my clients become recognized for what they experienced and what beauty they made with it.

That is what my heart experienced. It broke in a million places and in a million pieces. The last decade has been about painstakingly putting those pieces back together with gold. Now that the bowl is whole, restored with gold, and sturdy in its composition, it is ready to be put to use. It holds us now. It holds the aches and pains of everyday living. It processes every little thing that our little family goes through.

To be clear, just because my breaking led to a remaking, it doesn't mean we don't struggle. We do. Our two-address family has had another girlfriend come and go with the excitement and pain that process entails, tackled mental health issues, sorted out finances, buried grandparents, negotiated responses to COVID-19, shifted custody schedules, adjusted how things get paid for, trained a teenage driver, disagreed about faith, and navigated through a number of other important matters. The bowl holds us now. The work I did serves me and supports me through the endless number of issues I will face in my family. And although I *experienced* divorce, I am not divorced. I am a mother, a wife, and I am also a support to Mr. H.

People on the outside of your relationship with your former spouse probably won't understand the ways in which you attempt to work together. That's ok. Let them wonder. As you open yourself to these practices, you will find yourself doing all kinds of things you never imagined. I know a woman realtor who listed, marketed, and sold her former partner's home for him. I know another who made sure her newly arranged family's first joint Christmas after divorce was hosted at dad's new home so her kids could start to make meaningful memories there. I know a man who willingly does repairs at his former wife's home because it means his kids are supported. I know yet another who provides occasional childcare for her former husband's infant, who he had with another woman. As for me, I did laundry at Mr. H's home after his first new breakup. He gets car advice from my husband, and he gives my husband pointers about writing books.

Outsiders may wonder about your boundaries and question whether you are being careful. As insiders, we know the bigger thing we are striving for. We are claiming an integrated life for ourselves. It is a life that knows that a rising tide lifts all boats. Your life gets better when your former partner's life gets better. Their life benefits from your health as well.

Having a good divorce means becoming an expert at improvisational living. When the renowned Second City comedy club and school in Chicago trains new improv actors, they drill them on the most important phrase, which is "Yes, and...." You get up on stage and you start with the scene that you're married, and you pretend you are at home washing the dishes. Your improv partner comes on stage with this script starter and announces that you're going on a road trip to collect an old bike from a friend. As a beginning improv actor, you're going to want to steer the narrative back to what you had planned in your head. You might say, "No, I'm not going with you." As you grow in your craft, though, you learn to instinctively say, "Yes, and...." As in, "Yes, and...I have missed that bike so much!" Divorce can get thrown at you and the life you live after it will throw just as many new curve balls. "Yes, and..." consents to working with whatever comes your way. This opens you from resisting reality to working creatively with what's in front of you. You become up for anything and feel confident in your capacity to form an action plan.

One of the last things my Grandma Berry said to me before she died at age 99 was, "You don't get to be close to a hundred years old without learning how to bend with the wind." She couldn't give better advice. The impact of your divorce will cause enormous and fairly constant winds of change to blow at you. But you, as you piece together the bowl of your life again, are learning to bend. To say yes. To incorporate. To make space.

As we part ways, I send you forth into your great remaking. Trust that this pain is working on you, and for your family. Most of all, stay alert to all that is calling you toward growth, expansion, goodwill, and your ideal long game.

QUESTIONS FOR YOUR DEEPENING

1. What keeps you going?
2. What do you want your life to be about now, and going forward? Are you brave enough to leave the old narrative and start a new one?
3. What newness is crying out to you as you think about your life and post-divorce family in the next 12 months?

About The Author

Andrea Hipps, LBSW is a Certified Divorce Coach® and Certified Divorce Transition and Recovery Coach® who helps people all along the divorce continuum resolve their divorce debris and create beautiful two-address families for their kids. Her practice helps divorcing parents prevent drama on the front end, rework the story they have now, and create a life they can feel at home in. As a regular contributor to our nation's divorce recovery conversation, she's been featured on NBC, ABC, FOX, and the CW discussing how we can do divorce better for the sake of ourselves and our families.

More Support

Please visit my website to **download your free copy** of my "Practical Guide for Communicating with your Former Spouse Even When They're Difficult."

Stay Connected

Visit **www.andreahippsdivorcecoach.com** and sign up for my weekly divorce recovery email with tips, tricks, and mindset checks to keep you walking in a healthy direction.

Follow me on social:

Acknowledgments

It's hard to write about your divorce in a way that honors your former spouse and respects the stage of development of your children. I'm thankful my first husband, Shane Hipps, allowed this story to be told and blesses it as it makes its way to your hands.

To the authors I devoured along the way, who put words to tricky matters of the heart in an effort to make mine stronger.

To Judy Hahn, my spiritual director who first suggested that I could give something way bigger than I was losing.

To Sara Chambers of Elly and Nora Creative for the book cover design and for helping my business come to life in full color.

To every friend that held my hand through my decade of breaking and remaking: Amy "Wads" Anderson, Amie Jo "Shubby" Kreitzer, Jennifer Thomas, Sheila Yoder, Liz Brinkman, Miryam Lerma, Laura TenBrink, Tandy Champion, Jeanine Luciani, and Steph Bergsma. To my Soup Group and my FamWeCho. To Keri Mickelson, Chrisie Shrader, Erin Kempf, Allison Wedeberg, Emily Smith, Kristen Moore, and Christa Bird. You're all my boo-hoo crew. Thank you for seeing what I couldn't see and holding my hope when it got too heavy for me.

Acknowledgments

To my parents who have always stepped in, especially when I couldn't ask for it. Thank you for being the big people I asked you to be when this all started.

To Harper and Hadley, whose love for me is the most surprising and undeserved gift. You've lived this story alongside me and gave me a reason to make love bigger.

And to Todd. My Act II life with you is more than I imagined. Thank you for being big enough to let this story be part of our story. Thanks even more for writing a new one with me.

And to God, who convinced me that a bigger love was always available and to keep on until I found it.